God's Channel of Truth...

Is It The Watchtower?

by

E.B. Price

TEACH Services, Inc.
Brushton, New York

Copyright © 1999 TEACH Services, Inc.
ISBN 1-57258-163-8
Library of Congress Catalog Card No. 99-60963

Published by

TEACH Services, Inc.
254 Donovan Road
Brushton, New York 12916

God's Channel of Truth...

*Is It
The
Watchtower?*

Dedication

When I originally wrote this story in 1966, my Mother was a real source of encouragement and inspiration. She knew many of the people about whom this story is written and counted them among her dearest friends. She loved God and was happy to be numbered among those who "keep the commandments of God, and the faith of Jesus."

Tragically, she did not live to see this published. But her "works do follow" her. From my childhood she instilled in me a special desire to be of help to those who are confronted with the question, "God's Channel of Truth—is it the Watchtower?" As a young woman she had searched for truth and had found the answer to this question. To her memory I lovingly dedicate this little volume.

—The Author

A Word to the Reader

The setting of this story is Australia with its eucalyptus or gum trees and kangaroos. Readers who live in America or Europe will no doubt find this occasional "down under" flavor to be an added feature of interest.

As you follow the conversations, you may also draw conclusions as to the identity of "Bob Watson," and you will probably be right

However, though names of people and places have been altered for obvious reasons, and the dialogue reconstructed from many conversations, the experiences given are true. They actually happened to real people, many of whom, after over thirty years, are still living today

In this edition an extra chapter has been added to share with you the events that have happened to the leading characters in these intervening years.

— The Publishers

Contents

1
Trouble at "Blue Gums"

Lorna Stevens rearranged the Watchtower magazines and books neatly in the bookcase as she hurriedly dusted the furniture. Today she hoped to finish her work early, as she planned to spend the afternoon witnessing from door to door. As a faithful Jehovah's Witness, she happily anticipated her planned afternoon's activity, and the thought of it seemed to transport her miles away from the cares of "Blue Gums," the Australian farm, with its cows, pigs, and chickens. Even the sight of the hot summer sun already blazing down on the gum trees did not stifle her ardor. Rain, hail, or sun, Lorna would witness for Jehovah.

Suddenly she stopped, stood motionless, and listened. It was the sound of a car—the car of Clarice, her married daughter, coming up the driveway. Clarice had not called to say she was coming for a visit, so what could have brought her? Never mind, soon her daughter would tell her. Clarice was an open book: sincere, impetuous, honest. Any problem she had just bubbled out of her.

Mother and daughter had remained close to each other during the seven years Clarice had been married. But during the last year, since Clarice had been studying to become a Jehovah's Witness, the tie had become even closer. Especially was this so now that the daughter had made her decision to be baptized shortly and Paul, her husband, bitterly opposed her.

Clarice and four-year-old Gregory stepped out of the car. "You go talk with Grandpa," she told the boy. "See him over there by those trees?"

As Lorna and Clarice climbed the steps to the house, the mother sensed that something was wrong.

"Whatever is the matter, Clarice?" she asked. "You look as if something's bothering you."

"Well, Mum," Clarice began, "nothing's wrong—except you are going to be terribly disappointed in me. I am going to be a Seventh-day Adventist!"

"You can't be serious; you must be joking!" Lorna replied, puzzled and slightly shocked. She led the way into the living room where Nanna, her own mother, sat in her rocker.

"Sit down," Lorna invited. "We had better have a talk about all this, Clarice, for you don't make a decision like that overnight. Remember, one wrong decision will affect not only you, but also your children. And I'm sure you want to survive Armageddon."

Nanna, who had been a faithful Jehovah's Witness for many years, pulled her rocker a little closer to catch every word, as Clarice poured out the story of how a Bob Watson, a young Seventh-day Adventist minister, had called at her door. His visit lasted the whole afternoon, she said, and before he left she was convinced that Adventists have even more truth than do the Witnesses.

"But, Clarice," her mother remonstrated, "while Seventh-day Adventists can be nice people, like the Andersen, still they are not much different from the rest of Christendom. And, after all, what could you learn about them in just a few hours?"

"Everything, Mum."

Lorna shook her head and looked at Nanna, who was apparently too stunned to speak. It had taken both of these women twelve months, with the assistance of the congregation servant's wife, to teach Clarice the Witness teachings, and now she felt she knew all about Seventh-day Adventists in one afternoon!

"But, Mum and Nanna," she continued, "you don't understand. The Adventist teachings are so simple and clear, they come straight from the Bible. I've never seen anything like it in my life before. Every question I put to him, he found the answer in the Bible, and I could understand it just as it reads."

"Clarice"—Lorna spoke deliberately—"these people believe in the Trinity, that God is one person with a kind of three heads, which would mean that Jehovah died on the torture stake with Jesus Christ, and all that sort of confusion."

"Oh, no, they don't, Mum," Clarice answered. "That was the first thing I asked him, and he said Seventh-day Adventists have always believed and taught that the Father and Son are two distinct persons."

"Well, I don't know about that, but I do know they have it all twisted somehow, for I've talked to some of them."

"No, Mum!" Clarice disagreed. "We have lots more to understand about Jesus Christ and the work of the Holy Spirit in our lives. I took full notes on what he showed me from the Bible, and it is we that have it twisted, not they!"

"Where are these notes?"

"Down home," came the reply, "but I'll show them to you, Mum."

"Anyhow, what has worried you so much that you are thinking of leaving the truth?" Nanna asked.

"Don't think I just sold out easy. I really argued with him, and put him through his paces. In fact, I did not realize how much the Watchtower studies had taught me. I told him I believed that the Watchtower is God's channel for truth in the last days, and quoted Matthew 24:45, of the faithful and wise servant whom his master appoints to give spiritual food to the nations, just before Armageddon.

"Well, he told me he understood how I felt, because he himself had been interested in Watchtower teachings. But, he said, after studying deeply and thoroughly into its history, he had lost all confidence in the Watchtower. He said that down through the years the Watchtower has been altering its doctrines and teaching one thing and then another as truth. He said it has predicted so many dates that proved to be false prophecies that it is a sign that the Watchtower is not Jehovah's channel for truth. As Jesus said in Matthew 24, 'Believe it not.'"

"That's just a lot of exaggeration, Clarice," retorted Lorna. "It's typical of the way Christendom maligns the Watchtower! I can't bring to mind any dates in Watchtower publications that have proved false. Some teachings have been altered down through the years, but not many. What else did you hear?"

"Well, he explained that all the Ten Commandments are to be kept. Jehovah, instead of just giving one law, which was all done away at the torture stake, really had two kinds of laws. One was written on tables of stone which was taken and placed securely in the ark—the Ten Commandments, the moral code for all mankind. In the side of the ark was the other law, which contained blood sacrifices and ceremonies pointing forward to Christ. This was replaced by His ministry and death. Anyhow, I saw it all in the Bible, and I understand it clear as crystal!"

Lorna held her peace for the time being, though she felt she had never heard anything more ridiculous in her life. She encouraged Clarice to tell all the errors she had learned. In this way, the mother reasoned, she would know what she had to straighten out, and Nanna would be of good assistance too.

An hour and a half later, as the clock struck the hour of noon, the three women suddenly realized it was time for midday meals. If there was one thing Paul would not appreciate, it would be to return home and find that Clarice, his wife, had been out visiting, talking religion! Clarice collected Gregory from her father, and vanished in a quicker flurry than the one in which she had arrived.

Lorna never felt less like getting any meal ready. When it was over, she followed Nanna into the living room. Neither woman spoke at first. Then Lorna, wiping a tear from her eye, looked over at Nanna and said, "Mother, since you brought me into the truth years ago, all I've ever wanted was to see my children saved at Armageddon. Clarice has always been my black sheep, and just when I get her nearly right, the devil sends this along to wreck everything."

"Everything is not wrecked, Lorna. Jehovah's truth can withstand any test, and these religions have not got much to offer. Besides, I never heard so much nonsense in all my life as this business of putting two laws in the ark. The Bible tells of Noah's family and the birds and animals going into the ark, but definitely no books or tables of stone containing laws, much less the Ten Commandments. I had always felt these Adventists are strange people, but had no idea that they taught that!"

"Oh, Mother," her daughter exclaimed, "I don't really think for one moment that Clarice would become a Seventh-day Adventist. I'm sure we can knock that nonsense out of her head. But what frightens me is that she might lose her confidence in the Watchtower."

"You mean because of the dates and altered teaching, Lorna?"

"Yes, Mum. You know how Clarice is a stickler for a point. She just can't see how the Watchtower can change a truth, and yet it still remains truth. I fear she might stalemate with the Society teachings if she finds only one error the Watchtower has taught."

"Well, there are lots more than one, my dear, so if that is going to be Clarice's problem, we had better start to face it."

"Oh, Mother, things were never as bad as that, were they?" her daughter questioned.

"Not really. The Watchtower has been through a few patches; but then, so have God's people ever since He brought them out of Egypt and even before!"

Lorna looked at her watch. It was time for her to be moving, so she quickly dressed, packed her books and magazines in her satchel, and was soon driving to her first witnessing appointment.

Nanna assisted by looking after the younger children when they returned home on the school bus, but they all had been trained to prepare the evening meal on the days Lorna was out witnessing. They felt that in this way they, too, had a part.

John, Lorna's husband, was not a baptized Witness, but he never opposed her. He even attended some meetings and conventions with her and the family. He knew Lorna's religion was most important to her, and encouraged her in it.

Although Nanna had her own little cottage in the valley since she had been widowed, she spent more and more time in the happy atmosphere of Lorna's home. Despite the handicaps of increasing age, she found scores of little jobs she could do around the house and was a great help to the family.

On her way home that afternoon, Lorna had planned to call on Clarice. But she found an interested family, and spent so much time with them that she had to return directly home to arrive in time for tea. This interested family served as a tonic to Lorna's worried mind, and for a few hours she almost forgot the events of the morning. But as she drove home, Clarice's behavior began to come back to her, and she wondered what to do.

Evening chores finished, she decided to settle down to study on the history of the Watchtower. She took from the bookcase *Jehovah's Witnesses in the Divine Purpose*. She remembered reading it previously, but this time she determined to make a thorough and critical study so she could more readily defend the Watchtower.

When John called from the bedroom and asked her when she planned to come to bed, she was amazed to find it almost midnight. However, when she did get to bed, she lay awake for hours wrestling with her thoughts.

2
The Agreement

The work, worry, and lack of sleep of the day before made it hard for Lorna to get started on a new day. However, she arose early as usual, and set to work as energetically as possible doing her farm chores. When she had helped with the milking of the cows and had fed the pigs and chickens, she prepared breakfast for the family and saw the children off to school. Then she began on her housework, planning later to do further study.

Presently the telephone rang. It was Clarice, asking if her mother would be at home that afternoon. A visitor was planning to call, Clarice explained.

"Who is it?" her mother asked.

"Oh, you'll find out, Mum. He's visiting all the homes in the district."

"Not that young Adventist chap, is it?"

"Yes, Mum, it is. But you would not turn him from your door without giving him a hearing, would you?"

"I guess not," Lorna sighed. "Only I hope he does not think he can confuse me as easily as he did you, Clarice."

"Well, Mum, if you have the answers, then you ought to put him straight. He's a nice type of chap, and if you could convince him, he'd make a wonderful Witness."

That afternoon Lorna looked out the window and saw a young man drive up in his car. She usually went out to greet visitors to the farm, but this time she felt different. She had been warned of wolves in sheep's clothing that come in and spare not the flock. If Watson was one of these, she reasoned, even to tolerate him on the property was more than sufficient, without extending a welcome.

Bob Watson appeared to be younger than Lorna expected. In fact he looked like little more than a youth, hardly the age of her eldest son. He wore a simple gray suit and carried a bag of books, but had no clerical collar or preacher's accent.

His engaging smile and steady, honest-appearing eyes impressed her that here was a young man that must be shown the truth. Perhaps he could be rescued from Christendom.

She led him to the sitting room and introduced him to Nanna.

"Are you Reverend?" Nanna asked.

"Oh, no! In our church we never take that name. We are called simply pastor. But I'm a farmer's son, and when I'm visiting in farming communities, I like to be called plain Bob."

"Well, then," said Nanna, "all the neighborhood calls my daughter Mum, and I'm Nanna."

Lorna had not planned to be quite so friendly, but already she was warming to Bob, and besides, she knew Nanna was usually a good judge of character.

"What are you doing in this district, Bob?" Lorna asked.

"Well," he began, "I'm calling from door to door to tell people that what the Bible says is the 'end of the world' is soon to take place, and I tell people how to get ready."

"I did not know you people do any door-to-door work," Lorna observed. "You sound as if you'd make a good Jehovah's Witness, Bob."

"I know I would, Mum," Bob replied, "if I could have faith in the Watchtower and accept its teachings."

"What do you find wrong with the Watchtower, Bob?"

"To tell you the whole story, it started before I was born. My mother studied with the Bible Students, as they were called then, and considered joining the Society."

"What a pity she did not!" Lorna put in.

"She would have if she had felt it taught truth," Bob continued. "Only, at that time Judge Rutherford had changed nearly every teaching of Pastor Russell in some way, and in the confusion of the late twenties, Mother felt that the Society could not be God's channel for truth, and God's last warning message for the world. In fact, in less than ten years, an estimated 148 points of doctrine were changed, and this included many predicted dates which proved false. It all added up to her, especially in the light of Matthew 24:24, which warns about false prophecies in the last days, that she would have to look elsewhere for truth. Eventually she found it in the simple Biblical teachings of the Seventh-day Adventist Church."

"Bob, I know the Watchtower has altered certain teachings as it has come to a knowledge of greater truth, but don't you think you are exaggerating the facts to distort the picture?"

"Not at all. Let's have a look at the book the Watchtower published in 1917, called *The Finished Mystery*. This was the seventh volume of the 'Studies in the Scriptures' or the 'Millennial Dawn' series, and was the posthumous work of Pastor Russell. Judge Rutherford sold these by the hundreds of thousands during the early twenties. I guess you've seen it before, Mum?"

"As a matter of fact," Lorna confessed, "I haven't, although I've heard a lot about it, and I was even reading about it last night in one of our recent books, *Jehovah's Witnesses in the Divine Purpose*. Its release was described there as a 'bombshell' to Christendom, and I remember that chapters eleven to fourteen of this book outline the wonderful work its publication accomplished for the Society at the time of its reawakening after 1919."

"I think I've got it in the bottom of one of my trunks at home, Lorna," said Nanna. "I haven't looked at it for many, many years; but I believe it was one of the most outstanding books the Watchtower ever put out during the first fifty years of its history."

"Well, that's just it," said Bob. "This key book which the Watchtower put out as truth for so many years is today almost completely discarded by the Society in every detail and date. Yet the Watchtower has always claimed to be God's channel of truth for the last days."

"Oh, come now, Bob," answered Lorna, I don't think that could be right. Let me see these dates to start off with, and then we'll have a look at some of the teachings. So many false things are said, about the Watchtower that I insist that people prove every statement they make. And I'm afraid, Bob, that must apply to you!"

Jehovah's Witnesses in the Divine Purpose p.73–75 tells how ten million copies of this advertisement were distributed to assist in the sale of the 850,000 edition of *The Finished Mystery*

"I'll be happy to have that rule applied to me."

"Well, away you go, lad."

Bob picked up his copy of *The Finished Mystery* and began to thumb through its pages. "The earliest date in this book," he explained, "is 1874, which was stated to be the time of the second advent of Christ. You will find definite references to this throughout the book on pages 54, 60, 68, 71, 167, 368, 377, 386, and 395. This was taught as truth by the Watchtower for over fifty years, and then discarded. The same thing happened about the date 1878, which was also, for fifty years, said to be the time of the resurrection of the saints. Then the Watchtower decided it had made a mistake and set another date for the event. But the 1878 date is found throughout this volume, and you'll find references to it on pages 64, 182, 453, 539—"

"Oh, that will be enough for that one, Bob," cut in Lorna as she carefully jotted down each reference in her notebook. "And when do you reckon the Watchtower changed the date of the resurrection from 1878?"

"You'll find it in here," the young man replied a
the book *From Paradise Lost to Paradise Regained*
bookcase. He turned to page 192, where he read
30, with Lorna eagerly checking every word: 'O
many enlightening truths that God now gave His
was about the members of God's spiritual nation who had
died physically. This was in 1927. In that year the witnesses
understood that the dead spiritual Israelites had been raised
in 1918 to life in heaven with Christ Jesus. It was an invisible
resurrection, of course.'"

Lorna jotted that reference down too. "Have you any
more dates from *The Finished Mystery?*" she asked.

"Yes. Let's look at the year 1918, which was foretold as a
time when God would destroy the churches wholesale and
the church members by millions in a fearful revolution."

"I've never heard of that one in my life before!" put in
Lorna. "I think you'd better give me the references."

"Well, there are sufficient," said Bob confidently; "jot
down pages 398, 402, 404–405, 485, 513, and 515, while I
read to you some of the passages: '…in the year 1918, when
God destroys churches wholesale and the church members
by millions.' '…in the year 1918, when Christendom shall go
down as a system to oblivion, (Sheol) to be succeeded by
revolutionary republics.' 'Christendom shall be cut off in the
brief but terribly eventful period beginning in 1918 AD.....'"

"Then, there is the date 1920," Bob continued, "which the
Watchtower predicted would mark even the destruction of
the republics in a world-embracing anarchy, as described on
pages 179, 258, and 542."

"You've certainly done some study on this, Bob," Lorna
observed, as she finished copying down the last reference.

"Accepting Christ as my personal Saviour and following
truth is a life-and-death matter to me, Mum. The text that
says, 'My people are destroyed for lack of knowledge,' could
well apply to any of us. However, let's get back to some more
of these Watchtower dates."

"Have you still more?" Lorna inquired almost wearily.

"Oh, yes," Bob replied with obvious enthusiasm, "and
these are the most interesting of all—the date 1915, which

ater changed to 1925, and which foretold the setting up of the kingdom in Palestine. It is mentioned on page 128 of this book: 'There is evidence that the establishment of the Kingdom in Palestine will probably be in 1925, ten years later than we once calculated.'"

"This prophecy was later developed in the book Judge Rutherford wrote, entitled *Millions Now Living Will Never Die*. In fact, I have it with me, and I'll read it to you."

Bob pulled the green paperback out of his bag as Nanna remarked, "It's many years since I've seen one of those."

"Don't you have one of them at home, Mother?" Lorna asked.

"No," the elderly lady replied. "We burned all we could get hold of years ago. It was unfortunate that it was ever printed."

"Why?" Lorna asked, astounded.

Nanna shook her head. "Put that book away, Bob," she pleaded. "We are not really interested to hear what it says. That was years ago."

"But, Mother, I want to hear," Lorna retorted. "Go ahead, Bob. I'm going to get to the bottom of all this!"

"Well, here it is, then. It foretold the year 1925 as being the time when Abraham and others would be resurrected and the kingdom set up. I'll read it to you. The references are on pages 88 to 90 and again on page 97.

"The chief thing to be restored is the human race to life; and since other scriptures definitely fix the fact that there will be a resurrection of Abraham, Isaac, Jacob and other faithful ones of old, and that these will have the first favor, we may expect 1925 to witness the return of these faithful men of Israel from the condition of death, being resurrected and fully restored to perfect humanity and made visible, legal representatives of the new order of things on earth.'—Page 88. Then further: 'We may confidently expect that 1925 will mark the return of Abraham, Isaac, Jacob and the faithful prophets of old.'—Pages 89 and 90."

"Here is a photograph of the house Judge Rutherford built to entertain Abraham, Isaac, and the other princes when they were to be resurrected. He called it

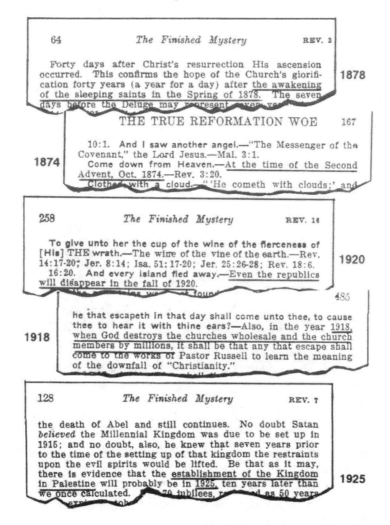

64   *The Finished Mystery*   REV. 3

Forty days after Christ's resurrection His ascension occurred. This confirms the hope of the Church's glorification forty years (a year for a day) after the awakening of the sleeping saints in the Spring of 1878. The seven days before the Deluge may represent seven ye... **1878**

THE TRUE REFORMATION WOE   167

1874   10:1. And I saw another angel.—"The Messenger of the Covenant," the Lord Jesus.—Mal. 3:1.
Come down from Heaven.—At the time of the Second Advent, Oct. 1874.—Rev. 3:20.
Clothed with a cloud.—"'He cometh with clouds;' and...

258   *The Finished Mystery*   REV. 16

To give unto her the cup of the wine of the fierceness of [His] THE wrath.—The wine of the vine of the earth.—Rev. 14:17-20; Jer. 8:14; Isa. 51:17-20; Jer. 25:26-28; Rev. 18:6.
16:20. And every island fled away.—Even the republics will disappear in the fall of 1920. **1920**

485

1918   he that escapeth in that day shall come unto thee, to cause thee to hear it with thine ears?—Also, in the year 1918, when God destroys the churches wholesale and the church members by millions, it shall be that any that escape shall come to the works of Pastor Russell to learn the meaning of the downfall of "Christianity."

128   *The Finished Mystery*   REV. 7

the death of Abel and still continues. No doubt Satan *believed* the Millennial Kingdom was due to be set up in 1915; and no doubt, also, he knew that seven years prior to the time of the setting up of that kingdom the restraints upon the evil spirits would be lifted. Be that as it may, there is evidence that the establishment of the Kingdom in Palestine will probably be in 1925, ten years later than we once calculated. 70 jubilees, reckoned as 50 years... **1925**

Some of the Watchtower Society's false dates and prophecies found in the book, *The Finished Mystery.*

'Beth-Sarim' which means 'House of the Princes.' It is still in San Diego, California, today."

Bob showed the photograph to Lorna.

"Is this genuine ?" she questioned.

"You would remember this book, would you, Nanna?" Bob asked, holding up the book *Salvation* he had brought with him.

"Yes," the old lady replied, "we published that at about the beginning of World War II."

"Well, here on page 312 is a drawing of Beth-Sarim, which is as you can see almost identical to this photograph taken recently. Under the heading 'Beth-Sarim' on page 311 it tells you all about the place, and how it had been built for the princes to occupy on their return. But unfortunately, the princes have never returned!"

Salvation, p. 311 tells how Beth-Sarim, "House of the Princes," was built in San Diego, California, USA to be occupied by Abraham, Isaac, Jacob and others mentioned in Hebrews 11, when they were to be resurrected to life on this earth.

Millions Now Living Will Never Die, p. 88–90 had prophesied that this would occur in 1925.

However, in *The Way to Paradise*, p. 224–228 it was stated that Abraham and the Princes would be in Jerusalem - (not California!) where one could call them on the telephone and arrange to have their loved ones progressively resurrected as they made the necessary preparations for them.

After Judge Rutherford had this mansion built, he took up residence in it "to await the arrival of the Princes". He died in it in 1942.

Bob handed the book to Lorna.

"Oh, so that's where that comes from," said Lorna. "Now things are beginning to add up. Last night I read in the *Divine Purpose* about the book *Millions*, and then read on page 110 a statement about the year 1925 proving a 'year of great trial to many of Jehovah's people.' Many, it said, left the Society and went back into the world."

"It was a big disappointment," Nanna conceded, "but on the other hand it did a lot of good. It got rid of those who would not remain loyal to the Watchtower."

"It certainly did," said Bob. "If I remember rightly from my study, during those years something like three quarters of the Bible Students lost their confidence in the Watchtower. About this time my own mother, observing all this confusion, realized that the Watchtower was not God's channel for truth and looked for a people that would teach pure Bible truth, free from the theories of men. This she found in the Seventh-day Adventist Church."

"But, Bob," Lorna objected, "God has to use men as His mouthpieces, and they are only human."

"Always remember," replied Bob, "when God uses men as His mouthpieces, He directs them by the Holy Spirit. Then they must give a clear message which is truth. Noah's message before the Flood, the messages given to Lot to leave Sodom, and warnings of Elijah, Isaiah, and Jeremiah were all clear-cut truth."

"But those men were prophets," Lorna countered. "Russell and Rutherford were not prophets."

"Well, Marley Cole, in his book, *Jehovah's Witnesses, the New World Society*, describes Charles T. Russell as 'Millennium's foremost prophet.'"

"Marley Cole's book is not an official Watchtower publication. I'm sure the Watchtower did not claim that."

Bob picked up the book *The Finished Mystery* again. Turning to page 378, he read that the Watchtower claimed Pastor Russell as the fulfillment of Ezekiel 2:5: "And they, whether they will hear, or whether they will forbear, (for they are a rebellious house,) yet shall know that there hath been a prophet among them."

"Well, I guess you can have prophets in the last days, just as in Bible times," suggested Nanna. "Although we don't usually refer to Pastor Russell and Judge Rutherford in this role, they were certainly used of Jehovah as His spokesmen through the Watchtower."

"Um," said Lorna slowly, "I can see our problem all right. If they were God's true spokesmen, then why did they make these mistaken prophecies or set wrong dates? Has that been your problem, Bob, as you have studied the Watchtower?"

"Yes," said Bob, "and the teachings likewise."

"Give us an example of some of the teachings you think have been in error," Lorna demanded.

"It is not I who say they were in error," the young man answered. "The Watchtower says it; otherwise they would not be teaching differently today. Take, for instance, this book, *The Finished Mystery*, which we know was considered paramount by the Watchtower. It is virtually a commentary on the prophecies of Revelation and Ezekiel, the applications of which are almost entirely discarded today by Watchtower publications. Also, the pyramid prophecies, and those which applied to the literal return of Israel to Palestine, are now rejected."

"So *you* think the 'bombshell' has exploded back on us, Bob?" Lorna chuckled good-naturedly.

"Well, Mum," said Bob, "you have told me I'd make a good Witness, but I'd want to be in an organization that has a solid foundation of truth. From its organization the Watchtower has claimed to be God's channel of truth. But the recurring problem to me is that if what the Watchtower once taught was truth, then it teaches error today. On the other hand, if it teaches truth today, then it has taught many errors during the major part of its history. That's not God's way of doing things."

"I don't think the Society claimed to be the channel of truth in the early days, Bob," Lorna suggested. "It is mainly since 1919 when Jehovah's spirit went forth and activated the Society to teach His truth."

"It is interesting to note, then," Bob replied, "that when this increased activity came, the book they sold by the hundreds of thousands was *The Finished Mystery*. On page 144 this book declares, 'The WATCHTOWER BIBLE AND TRACT SOCIETY is the greatest corporation in the world, because from the time of its organization until now the Lord has used it as His channel through which to make known the Glad Tidings.' So that makes yet another difficulty to be sorted out."

"It all adds up to this, then," Lorna summarized, "if I can get these problems sorted out for you, then you'll become a Jehovah's Witness?"

"If you can convince me that the Watchtower is God's channel of truth, the way of salvation, and teaches Bible truth, then I certainly will, Mum," Bob agreed. "On the other hand, if I can show you that Seventh-day Adventists follow the truth, then will you follow the Lord and become an Adventist?"

Lorna Stevens burst out laughing at the thought, but she admired Bob's earnestness. "Bob, if you convince me that Seventh-day Adventists have the truth, I'll not only be one, but I'll give you a prize sucking pig!"

"You might as well make it your prize sow, Bessie, and be done with it," said Nanna, joining in the joke.

Bob smiled and rose to leave. "Let's allow the Holy Spirit to lead us," he said, and bade the ladies goodnight.

When Bob's car had disappeared, the two ladies were still smiling at the suggestion of their being anything but faithful Jehovah's Witnesses.

Then John, Lorna's husband, came into the house. He had overheard Bob's last remarks and asked, "What is this I hear about you going to become Seventh-day Adventists?"

"Oh!" exclaimed Lorna, "we've got no intentions of becoming Adventists. We were just joking with that minister of theirs."

"So that's it," he said.

"He may have problems believing in the Watchtower as the channel of truth," added Lorna, "but we'll unravel it all, for we do have the truth, and it comes to us through the Watchtower!"

3
1914 and All That!

Mum, you seem anxious to get things finished early tonight," Gary said, as the family sat down to their evening meal.

"Well, Son," Lorna answered, "Nanna and I are slipping over to her place tonight for a few minutes."

"What for?" Mary added.

"Because Nanna has some old Watchtower books in a trunk, and she's going to let me have them."

"Oh, that will be good, Mummy," said the youngest. "I'll carry them with me next time I go out witnessing with you."

"Well, I don't know about that," said Lorna hesitatingly. "I think the newer publications are best for people today."

"But the Bible's old, and we take it," he replied.

Lorna made no further comment, but the words 'the Bible is old, and we take it' kept ringing in her ears. She thought of how God said of Himself, "I am Jehovah; I have not changed." Yet she had been challenged that very day with her own Watchtower publications whose contents had been changed radically in the space of a few short decades.

Two hours later, Lorna and Nanna returned. By that time the younger children had done their homework and gone to bed. Valmai, who had finished school and was working on a nearby farm during the day, came out to the car to meet her mother and grandmother.

"What a lot of books you have!" she exclaimed. She helped her mother carry them into the house, while Nanna made her way, assisted only by her walking stick.

"Be careful, Val, of that book on top of the pile," Lorna called to her. "That's the book I especially went over for."

Valmai glanced down at it as she stepped into the light of the kitchen, and read the title: *The Finished Mystery*. "I've never seen this before that I can remember," she remarked.

She left the books on the living-room table, then excused herself to retire.

Nanna began to knit quietly. Lorna reasoned that with John away at a district meeting she should have a good night's study, uninterrupted, to check up on all Bob had said that afternoon.

Less than half an hour later she heard the familiar sound of Clarice's car coming up the driveway. She wished she had more time to look over the books so she could straighten out Clarice. But, on the other hand, she also longed to see her and have a good talk.

Clarice came in looking very pleased with herself. She explained how Paul had been called to another farm to help a neighbor for the evening. She got a baby-sitter in, and that meant she could get away for a couple of hours.

"Well, Mum," she began, "how did you get on with Bob today ?"

"Oh," said Lorna, "he's a nice enough chap, and very sincere, but he expected me to believe all he said!"

"Well, did you?"

"Of course not. But I was just checking up on him now, as Nanna happened to have some of the old books. We slipped over to her cottage this evening and got them."

"What are you finding?"

"So far, I've found what he said is right," her mother admitted.

"Well, Mum, I've not been able to fault him yet. He called on me again this morning for a few minutes to leave me a book, and we had some more discussion."

"There's only one thing about Bob and those dates," Lorna observed. "I noticed when he was listing all the prophecies connected with dates, which he said proved false, that there is one he carefully avoided mentioning—1914. This is one date that Christendom cannot gainsay, and after all that is the real foundation of our Watchtower teachings.

"The date 1914 is when the 'Gentile times' ended, the 'time of the end' began, Christ's second coming into the kingdom took place, and also when Satan was cast out of heaven. This is the basis of the Society's teachings, not those other dates like 1874 or 1925 that Bob quoted. So my faith remains unshaken."

"But, Mum," objected Clarice, "didn't he explain to you that 1914 is both historically out in its reckoning, and without Scriptural foundation besides?"

"How?" asked her mother, unbelieving.

"You know how in the *Paradise* book it explains that the 2,520 years of the 'times of the Gentiles' began in 607 B.C., when the theocracy finished and Zedekiah the last king of Judah had his eyes put out and was taken prisoner to Babylon by Nebuchadnezzar; and it ended thus, in 1914?"

"Yes," said Lorna hesitantly.

"But it did not begin in 607 B.C. at all, for Zedekiah was taken prisoner not in 607 B.C., as the Watchtower teaches, but in 586 B.C., over twenty years later. So the whole date of 1914, based on the 2,520-year prophecy of Watchtower publications, collapses!"

"Now, don't you be too hasty, Clarice," her mother counseled. "Just let us make sure, and we'll check exactly what the *Paradise* book says too."

For some time Lorna examined *Paradise*, until she had marked pages 103 and 172–173. "I've got it all here," she announced as she began to examine the statements. "It says that Nebuchadnezzar took Zedekiah off the throne of Judah in 607 B.C. clearly enough. Now what do you say is wrong with that?"

"It did not happen then, Mum. It happened in 586 B.C. Every reliable historical source will tell you that. I made a special trip to the library to check it up."

"Those sources are probably biased."

"But, Mum," Clarice added, "one authority even quoted recent archaeological evidence discovered on the tablet known as V.A.T. 4956, in the Berlin Museum, which proves beyond all doubt that 586 was the correct date, and not 607 as taught by the Watchtower." Clarice presented her mother with a list of references and quotations she had jotted down.

"I think I'd like to check it up for myself," she said as she reached for a copy of *Smith's Bible Dictionary*. "We've used this for years in our Society meetings to check on things, so I'll be interested to see what it says."

She took it from the bookcase and looked up the section on "Zedekiah." "Here it is," she announced confidently, and read, "'Zedekiah was but twenty-one years old when he was thus placed in charge of an impoverished kingdom, 597 B.C. His history is contained in a short sketch of the events of his reign given in Second Kings 24:17 to 25:7.' There you are! That does not say 586 B.C., but I'm sure when we work it all out, we'll find that the date is 607 B.C., when we add on the years he reigned before he was captured."

"But this is B.C., not A.D., Mum," Clarice explained. "Remember, we have to count backward, not forward."

"Oh, yes," her mother admitted, "I'm getting all tangled up. In that case, then, we could be wrong. But let us also look up Second Kings 25 from the Bible and check every detail carefully."

Clarice picked up a small maroon-covered King James version of the Bible published by the Watchtower, and turned to the chapter. She read the first verse, which mentioned that Nebuchadnezzar besieged Jerusalem in the ninth year of Zedekiah's reign, and noticed that the Bible had the date 588 B.C. in the margin next to it. Then, in the verses which followed, it told of the city's being taken two years later. Zedekiah then had his eyes put out and was carried to Babylon in the eleventh year of his reign.

Lorna and Nanna carefully checked and rechecked all the statements and passages in silence.

"There you have it, Mum," said Clarice. "*Smith's Bible Dictionary* says Zedekiah began to reign in 597 B.C. and the Bible says he was captured in the eleventh year of his reign, which would be 586 B.C. Then this Bible published by the Watchtower has the year 588 B.C. in the margin for the time the city was besieged, and it was taken two years later, which brings us again to 586 B.C."

"Fancy two Watchtower publications contradicting each other like this!" Lorna exclaimed. "What do you think, Mother?"

"What can one think?"

"That's not all, though, Mum," Clarice continued. "The 2,520-year period is applied from the prophecy of Daniel 4, concerning the 'seven times' or seven years Nebuchadnezzar was insane, reckoning seven years to have 2,520 days, each day representing a year. However, in Daniel 4 there is no connection between Nebuchadnezzar and any future fulfillment after his time, because in Daniel 4:28 the Bible says, 'All this came upon the king Nebuchadnezzar.' Again, in verse 33, 'The same hour was the thing fulfilled upon Nebuchadnezzar.' If the Bible says it was fulfilled on Nebuchadnezzar, then it is unscriptural to apply it, as we have been taught by the Watchtower, to a later time period, completely unrelated to Nebuchadnezzar. So 1914 is both historically and Scripturally incorrect."

"Oh, Clarice," said Lorna, feeling a little exasperated. "What next are we going to be confronted with? I just wish we'd never met this Bob!"

"However, Mum," said Clarice, "the 1914 teaching of events connected with the second 'coming' or *parousia* of Christ Jesus into His kingdom, also cannot be reconciled with the Bible teaching on at least six counts."

"Now first of all, Clarice, what do the Adventists believe about the *parousia*?" Lorna asked.

"This is what they believe, Mum." Clarice pulled out of her handbag a small book entitled *Our Lord's Return*, which featured on the front cover a picture of a literal and visible return of Christ with the angels in the clouds of heaven. "They believe this will happen at Armageddon."

"Oh, I could never believe that!"

"But, Mum, have a look at some of these Bible texts. What about the one in Revelation 1:7, where it says 'Every eye shall see Him'?"

"Yes, but that is the spiritual eye of understanding only. When the *parousia* took place in 1914, it was the spiritual eyes of the faithful Watchtower servants who discerned that His presence had taken place."

Clarice gave a puzzled frown, then asked, "Mum, if that was so, why was it that three years later, in 1917, the Watchtower put out a book still maintaining that Christ's second advent had taken place in 1874?"

Lorna was silent as she thought for a few moments of *The Finished Mystery*.

"Another thing, Mum, in Matthew 24:30 our *New World Bible* says, 'And then the sign of the Son of man will appear in heaven, and then all the tribes of the earth will beat themselves in lamentation, and they *will see* the Son of man coming on the clouds of heaven with power and great glory." All the tribes of the earth do not have spiritual understanding, but they see Him. It makes you begin to wonder if it is not a literal coming, after all.

"There's another passage, too, that's a problem. It is found in First Thessalonians 4:15 to 17, where it describes how at the Lord's presence or coming, He descends from heaven with the voice of an archangel, a commanding call, and a sound of God's trumpet, and the dead in Christ rise right then. These will be caught up in the clouds along with those who are living at that time, and thus they will meet the Lord in the air. It seems to me with all that announcement and noise that everybody will know about it, and that it would not have happened in 1914."

"Well, Clarice, first of all you have to understand that those resurrected are only the 144,000 class who were taken to heaven then. And it was, of course, an invisible resurrection."

"But, Mum, if the 144,000 class were resurrected then, why weren't all the 144,000 class who were living on the earth then, 'together with them …caught away in the clouds to meet the Lord in the air' just as the Bible says? They would have suddenly disappeared, then, but of course that did not happen either in 1914."

"Oh, Clarice," her mother exclaimed, "it is not as simple as all that. You ought to read more Watchtower books, and then you would understand it all clearly."

"But, Mum, I've been reading Watchtower publications solidly now for a whole year, and nothing makes sense of the Bible, like that which I've learned in the last few days from the Adventists. Here's another one," Clarice continued. "According to Second Thessalonians 2:8 the wicked are going to be destroyed by the brightness of the *parousia*, or coming. How did that happen in 1914?"

"Well, it did in a spiritual way. As the good news of the kingdom was taken to the nations in brilliance and triumph, the wicked who rejected it passed the eternal death sentence on their own heads, so that in this way they are being destroyed by the good 'news' of His 'presence.'"

"Mum, do you really think this Watchtower explanation is satisfactory? Apart from the fact that they did not know for a number of years after 1914 that Christ's presence had taken place, elsewhere in the Bible (such as Luke 17:26 to 30 and Matthew 24:36 to 39) the 'presence,' 'coming,' or 'revealing' of the Son of man is likened to the day that Lot went out of Sodom and it was destroyed, or when Noah went into the ark and the Flood came and swept them all away. It describes it as something sudden and unexpected by the wicked, which sweeps them all together into a destruction which sounds like Armageddon. The more I've looked up all the texts, the more I'm afraid the Adventists are right. I'm sure all this did not happen in 1914, but is still future."

"Give me a list of these texts, please, and I'll study them after you are gone," Lorna said, as she picked up her notebook and pencil again.

"Well, I'll give you a few more, Mum, and then I had better get moving just in case Paul comes home earlier than expected. In fact, I think I'll leave this book with you and you can check the texts it mentions too. Now, where was I up to? I've mentioned 'every eye' seeing Him, the resurrection of the dead, the translation of the living, and the destruction of the wicked; that all takes place when Christ comes, but did not happen in 1914. Oh, I know, there's the point about the holding of the Memorial service, or what the churches call the 'communion' service.

"The Bible says, in First Corinthians 11:26, that this service is to be held, until He comes or, as our Bible says, 'until he arrives.' If Christ became present in 1914, then why do we still hold the Memorial service each year?"

"Well," said Lorna wearily, "what is the reference and I'll look that one up too."

"There is just one other point I want to leave with you, Mum, on this subject: If Christ Jesus began ruling in 1914, then He would have finished His work as our High Priest, as described in the book of Hebrews, where 'He ever giveth to make intercession' for its. As our Bible renders it in Hebrews 7:25, 'Consequently he is able also to save completely those who are approaching God through him, because he is always alive to plead for them.' If He began the work of ruling, and finished His work of being our mediator and pleading to save us, then no one could be saved since 1914?"

Clarice looked at her watch, and almost before Lorna knew what bad happened, her daughter was gone.

Lorna sat like one in a trance. She had intended to straighten Clarice out, but instead, Clarice was—what *was* Clarice doing to her, anyway? Nanna shook her head without comment; then she excused herself and made her way to bed. With a troubled heart, Lorna was left alone to check and recheck the texts Clarice had mentioned and the problems she had posed.

Later she began reading the little book Clarice had left, on the teaching of the Adventists about Christ's return. She compared its contents with her own Watchtower publications. To say the least, she found herself confused.

John arrived home late from his meeting, and for that Lorna was grateful, though she felt very tired. John took one look at the table covered with books and asked, "What have you been doing with all those books, honey? Are you frightened of losing that prize sow of yours?"

"I'd willingly give the old sow away and all her piglets with her, if we wouldn't be worried by that young Adventist preacher!" She tried bravely to smile.

"Cheer up, honey." John placed his arms protectively around her. "I'll not let any of these Adventist preachers hurt you!"

"And then the sign of the Son of man will appear in heaven, and then all the tribes of the earth will beat themselves in lamentation, and *they will see* the Son of man coming on the clouds of heaven with power and great glory." Matthew 24:30.

"For the Lord himself shall descend from heaven with a shout, with the voice of the archangel, and with the trump of God: and the dead in Christ shall rise first: then we which are alive and remain shall be *caught up together with them* in the clouds, to meet the Lord in the air: and so shall we ever be with the Lord." 1 Thessalonians 4:16–17

"Oh, John, he's really a nice young chap, and in fact you'd like him. But a fellow with his knowledge ought to be a Jehovah's Witness."

"Then he wouldn't put the Ten Commandments in Noah's ark!" John teased.

"Oh, Nanna and I have not tackled him on that yet. We are keeping it up our sleeves, but we have it ready for him."

"Well, make it an evening visit when you do, as I'd like to be present and enjoy the fun! Poor fellow, I may have to protect him from all three of you." John laughed at his own joke, but Lorna felt more serious about the matter.

"Where is it all going to end?" she kept asking herself, "and will it finally strengthen our faith in the Watchtower?"

4
Here or Near?

The Stevens family were astir with Watson's challenge to their Watchtower beliefs. However, the eldest married son, David, and his wife, Brenda, who were faithful Witnesses, lived in another district. Although Clarice would like to have sent Bob to see them, she refrained, complying with her mother's wishes.

John, Lorna's husband, took an easygoing attitude toward the debate, as he felt it did not affect him. In the meantime he continued to manufacture jokes, though these were not always appreciated. Having heard Mum and Nanna talk about the Ten Commandments being written on tables of stone and placed in Noah's ark, John talked about the "stones" in the ark, then the "stones" in the "boat," and finally the "bricks in the boat!" The children took up the saying also.

"Mum, when are you going to get the bricks out of the boat for Bob?" they asked. All the family enjoyed the joke, but Lorna felt she wanted to straighten out the *parousia* and 1914 before she tackled anything else. Then the "bricks in the boat" could serve for the final knockout.

As Lorna studied the subject on both sides, she came to a conclusion: Adventists teach that Christ's visible coming or presence is *near*, while the Watchtower teaches that Christ's invisible presence is *here*. So she arranged with Bob to come and discuss the matter thoroughly the next Monday night.

When Clarice heard about it, she made sure she would be able to be there, and Nanna slept in the afternoon so she, too, could enjoy the evening. Even John found that curiosity had gained the better of him, and he made some excuse for missing his usual district meeting that night. When Bob arrived, he found quite an audience in the living room gathered around the old family table.

He set up a little blackboard he had brought, placed his books on the table, then bowed his head and offered a short prayer. He explained he always did this before he opened the

Bible, to ask that the Holy Spirit might teach and guide into all truth.

Looking up from his prayer, he began, "Now tonight we have arranged to study the subjects of—"

"The bricks!" put in Gary. Mary gave a muffled chuckle. John nudged him under the table and whispered, "Another night!"

Lorna, not wanting to take time for explanations, added, "It was the *parousia*, Bob, the coming of Christ, as you call it. Is Christ's presence here, or is it yet future?"

"I think that in order to understand the differences of belief on this subject, it is best for us to go back in our history," Bob explained. "This would take us back to the year 1844, when many people thought Christ would return literally, and were disappointed when He did not come. These people broke up into many groups. Some gave up religion. Others went on setting further dates. But there were a few who decided to study into exactly what the Bible says on the subject. They came to the conclusion that Christ still will come, but that no one knows the day nor the hour. They decided that setting dates is unscriptural. As they studied further they discovered other lost Bible truths taught and practiced by the early Christian church. In 1863 they organized themselves into what is known today as the Seventh-day Adventist Church. These people have never set a date for Christ's return, and they have always believed His future return will be literal and visible.

"On the other hand, a group of Second Adventists continued to set dates, predicting October, 1874, as the time for Christ's return. Pastor Russell attended one of their meetings, conducted by a Jonas Wendell in 1872, and accepted this teaching. However, when Christ did not come in 1874, Russell and the group of date setters were very disappointed, until two years later a Mr. Barber explained that Christ had really come in 1874, but that it was an invisible coming. He took his cue from the *Emphatic Diaglott*, which translates 'coming' in Matthew 24:27, 37, and 39, as 'presence,' from the Greek word *parousia*."

Bob read the story from *The Finished Mystery*, pages 53 and 54, and also, though in lesser detail, from *Jehovah's*

Witnesses in the Divine Purpose, on pages 14 and 15. Lorna and Nanna checked him from their copies of those books.

"Well, now," Bob continued, "for the next fifty years, from 1874, the Watchtower taught that Christ's second advent took place in 1874 and He has been present since that time. The official title given to the Society's paper during the time was known as *Zion's Watchtower and Herald of Christ's Presence.* In fact, during, this time, as outlined on pages 68 and 71 of *The Finished Mystery,* all the signs mentioned by Christ in the Gospels and elsewhere in the Bible were applied by the Watchtower as proving Christ's presence from 1874."

Bob drew a time line on his blackboard to cover the ninety years and more from 1874 to our present decade. He filled in the time from 1874 to the mid-1920's. During this time the Watchtower taught that Christ had been present since 1874.

"Now," Bob continued, filling the rest of the time graph, "for the last forty-some years the Watchtower has taught that Christ's presence took place in 1914, and all of the signs are now applied since that time to prove His presence in the world. Now, I ask you, which teaching is right and which is wrong?"

"What the Watchtower now teaches is the truth, Bob," Lorna replied. "In these last days it has been given greater light. Now we understand that since 1914 Christ has been invisibly present."

"But don't you think it strange that, if God is leading the Watchtower, He would have allowed it to teach error for fifty of its ninety years? However, I do not feel this is the only problem, for nowhere in the Bible does it say the signs indicate that Christ is here, but that His presence or coming is *near.*"

"Well," said Lorna, "I think it all goes back to one's translation of the Greek word *parousia.* Some translations have it as 'presence,' and others make it an 'arrival' or 'coming.' You have learned Greek and say one thing, Bob, and our books say another. Who is to know what it should be?"

"Me!" said John.

"Oh, don't be silly, John!" Lorna remonstrated. "You've never learned a Greek word in your life!"

"But there is Tony, who lives just across the paddock. He has only recently come from Greece. He would tell us. I'll go over and get him!"

John quickly excused himself and soon returned with Tony. "Tony," John asked, "what does *parousia* mean?"

Tony looked at them helplessly and shrugged his shoulders.

Bob wrote it on the blackboard in English letters, then in Greek ones.

Tony took one look at it and exclaimed, "It is *parousia*!" He gave the word a slightly different pronunciation than the others had. "You want the mean of this word?"

"That's right," John encouraged.

"It something wonderful very much, what all can the very much see. Say, the Queen of England, well she come to Australia. Everybody happy and go see her driving along the street, and she looking the very much beautiful, and they shout and wave. Then that is *parousia*. You now understand me?"

"If they don't, I do," said John. He thanked Tony for coming and went to the door with him.

"Tony's description is pretty close to the Adventist idea of Christ returning in glory, amid shouts and trumpets and the like," observed Clarice.

"Perhaps," said her mother, "but I'm beginning to get sick of ideas of this church or that one. All I want is truth, pure truth, straight from the Bible!"

"That would be a good thing," Bob agreed.

"Now, the problem as I see it," said Valmai, "is to decide whether the signs indicate the *parousia* is here or near?"

"What chapter is it in Matthew that tells about the signs, Mum?" asked Clarice. "It's chapter 24, isn't it?"

All those present looked up that passage in their Bibles—all except John, that is, who still tried to look indifferent.

Bob suggested that they read Matthew 24:30, 31, so Mary began reading from her New World Bible. "'And then the sign of the Son of man will appear in heaven, and then all the tribes of the earth will beat themselves in lamentation, and they will see the Son of man coming on the clouds of heaven with power and great glory. And he will send forth his angels with a great trumpet sound, and they will gather his chosen ones together from the four winds, from one extremity of the heavens to their other extremity.'

"Nothing could be clearer that, when Christ comes, all including the wicked, who have no eyes of spiritual understanding, will see Him literally in His glory and with all the angels," observed Bob. "But let us read on."

Valmai read this time: "'Now learn from the fig tree as an illustration this point: Just as soon as its young branch grows tender and it puts forth leaves, YOU know that summer is near. Likewise also YOU, when YOU see all these things, know that he is near at the doors.'"

"What does 'all these things' mean?" John asked.

"It means the signs mentioned in this chapter," Lorna replied.

"Oh, then the whole thing is so clear that even a blind man could see it. These signs show that Christ's coming is *near*." John picked up Gary's New World Bible and examined the passage again. "Why, it says He is *near* at the doors."

"I can see it too, Dad," Clarice agreed. "A person is not present here in this house until he has come through the door. Christ's presence will soon take place, but it has not yet; which means it could not have taken place back in 1874 or 1914."

"Another point, too," added Bob, "is the fact that the signs are sent to warn us to be ready for His presence or coming, as in verses 42 and 44. It is too late if His *parousia* has already taken place. And in verses 36–41 we are told no one will know when it will take place. When it does, it will be like the Flood which came suddenly and swept all the wicked to destruction. In fact, we are told about two people grinding at the mill, or in the field. One is saved and the other abandoned or destroyed."

Lorna read and reread the passages, but she said nothing.

"Well, it is clear to me," said John, "that the coming or whatever you call it is still future."

"In fact," said Bob with a kindly smile, "the Bible, right here in this chapter, warns us about people in the last days who say Christ is here. Look at verse 23: 'Then if anyone says to YOU, "Look! Here is the Christ," or, "There!" do not believe it.'"

"Look at this copy of *Awake* that I was reading the other day," said Valmai. She reached over to the bookcase and held a copy up. "See, here is the leading article with the title 'Christ Is Present!' What do you think of that?"

"No problem at all, Valmai," Clarice replied. "You've Just had your answer. The Bible says, 'Believe it not.'"

"So you really think we are wrong?" Nanna asked Bob. "And you are quite worried about our believing Christ is present now?"

Bob paused a moment, his deep concern evident. "To me," he began, "it is a real tragedy not to understand the great truth of the return of our Lord and Saviour Jesus Christ. It should be the hope and joy of every Christian, to meet Him personally and live with Him throughout eternity. However, I am most concerned that we accept Christ's death for us on Calvary as an atonement for our sins. When we accept Him thus as our personal Saviour, then by the indwelling power of the Holy Spirit, we want to stop sinning, to stop breaking His laws. We desire to please Him, to keep the commandments."

"The bricks, the bricks!" Gary burst forth. "Come on, Mum, now we can get them!"

"Not tonight, Son." John looked at his watch. "It is well past your bedtime, but perhaps if Bob would like to come back next Monday night, we'll see about them then."

"What bricks are you talking about, Dad?" Clarice seemed to realize there was a family joke she didn't know about.

"Oh, that can keep until next Monday night, Clarice. We'll tell you all about it then."

5
Father to the Rescue

Early Sunday morning Clarice called her father on the telephone to say she was in trouble. "Dad, Paul and I have had a real upset this morning. He says he won't let me come over tomorrow night for the study. Do you think you could talk to him today? Paul usually takes more notice of you than anyone."

"What's it worth, Clarice?"

"A bar of chocolate."

"I'll settle for a pack of cigarettes!"

"No, Dad. They'll only give you lung cancer. Chocolate it is!"

"You win," laughed John. "That's a deal."

Paul had been having trouble with his cows, and milk production was down, so John offered to investigate the trouble.

Together they began a tour of the farm to inspect the milking shed, water holes, pastures, and individual cows.

"We are going to have some fun tomorrow night, Paul," John said as they made their way to the milking shed. "This young Adventist fellow has been stirring the womenfolk up, and everyone is talking religion. Tomorrow night is the grand finale."

"Oh, you poor fellow, Pop. Nothing makes me mad faster than to have religion for breakfast, dinner, and tea."

"The Witnesses are all right, Paul," said John. "You just have to know how to live with them and keep them happy."

"Well, they don't keep me happy. I could blow a fuse every time I think of them."

"What's your problem?" asked John.

"Well, first it is this blood transfusion business. I can't think that God who healed the sick and raised the dead wants innocent children to die for want of a transfusion."

"I've never been very happy about it either," agreed his father-in-law. "I always thought I'd wait and see if any of the children needed one. Then if Lorna would not give permission for it, I would. It's not worth getting upset over, though, for it may never happen to your children."

"What about Clarice? If she needed a transfusion and refused it, I'd be left without a wife, with small children to bring up. I reckon it's all wrong to say it would be 'the will of God' for her to die. What has eating blood to do with placing blood in veins to save a life?"

"It all seems wrong to me too," John agreed, "but still you get nowhere by arguing. If that is the Watchtower interpretation of those Bible texts, they accept it without question. It's not the people in the Witness organization who are to blame. There are some very nice people in it. The trouble is that their headquarters tells them what to do, and they do it without question."

"I suppose that's why they regard themselves as persecuted, Pop? They are told they must be right because they are persecuted for their beliefs. But we all know that Communists, nationalists, and many others have died for their beliefs. And if religious persecution were the test of truth, then we should all be Jews because so many millions of them died under Hitler."

"Well, I don't care who people are or what they believe. I admire anyone who has the courage to die for his faith. I know some of the Witnesses have, but I do think they ought to examine carefully what they are dying for, first."

By this time John had half of the milking equipment disassembled, while Paul assisted him. For a time they said little, but eventually Paul broke the silence. "Do you think there is anything in this religion business, Pop?"

"Well, yes, I do," John answered. "They've all got something, but I don't know who's got the most. The Witnesses are about the nearest I've seen yet, but even then, I think the Watchtower has led them for too much of 'a dance' down through the years."

"Oh," commented Paul, "how do you mean?"

"I'll give you an example," said John, picking up a spanner and tightening some bolts. "Take this business of what happens when a person dies. Nearly all the churches teach that one either goes straight to heaven or to hell. Well, I reckon they don't really believe it themselves, the way they mourn and carry on when a loved one is supposed to be enjoying heavenly bliss! Now the Witnesses have got something when they say from the Bible that death is a sleep, and everybody sleeps in death until the resurrection at the last day. But then they spoil it all by adding their own Watchtower interpretation to it."

"How do you mean, Pop?"

"Well, for years they taught that in 1878 a whole crowd of them were resurrected and went to heaven in spirit form. Later they realized they'd made a mistake on that one, and moved the date up to 1918. Since then a certain heavenly class go straight to heaven as soon as they die, which in my opinion is a real shame, for this teaching makes Witnesses believe the same as the rest of Christendom.

"In fact, all this chopping and changing of dates has caused them some real embarrassment too. I had a bit of fun with Lorna last night over something I discovered in an old Watchtower book of theirs called *The Finished Mystery*. I found where the Watchtower claimed that when Russell died he went to heaven in 1916 and continued managing the Society from up there. At first Lorna would not believe they had ever taught such a thing, until I showed her the statements, on pages 144 and 420. Then I asked her what would have happened when Judge Rutherford died and arrived in heaven in 1942 to continue his work, as those two did not get on too well together. And to make matters worse, just after Russell died, Rutherford set about changing his teachings!

"Then I could not resist asking her how Russell got on in heaven in 1916, when the Watchtower decided in 1927 that the resurrection did not take place until 1918. Russell had, according to their own publications, already been in heaven for two years!

"Poor Lorna, I guess I shouldn't have done it, as she's taken a bashing this last week or so."

"What did she say?" asked Paul.

"Oh, she just said, 'John, whatever you do, keep your mouth shut about this and don't tell that young Adventist preacher what you've found.' However I don't think you could tell Bob much about the Watchtower that he doesn't know. He reckons he'd be a Witness if it taught all the truth, and he's mighty sure it doesn't."

"This young preacher must know his stuff!" Paul exclaimed.

"Why don't you come up and bring Clarice tomorrow night? He's coming up, and Lorna and Nanna reckon they are going to 'clean him up' over a point or two. Since I've never seen him lose a round yet, it's going to be mighty interesting."

"But I told her this morning she couldn't go."

"Forget it, Paul!" laughed John. "You'll have the fun of your life, and it will do you both good."

"It's a date, then," he agreed, and walked over to fetch the bucket of milk his father-in-law was about to test.

When they returned to the house for lunch, Clarice greeted them. "I hope you men are really hungry."

"Hungry? There's just nothing I'd like more than a nice bar of chocolate!" said her father.

"Have you earned it, Dad?"

"Sure thing!" His eye twinkled.

When John arrived home that night, he told Lorna that Paul planned to attend tomorrow night's study and bring Clarice.

"Wonderful!" his wife enthused. "I'm glad Paul will be here. I just know that Nanna and I will put Bob in his place, and we'll all know for sure that the source of truth is the Watchtower."

6
Bricks in the Boat?

"Mum, is tonight the night you get the bricks out of the boat?" asked Gary at breakfast.

"That's right, Son," said Lorna. "But please keep it to yourself. Don't advertise it to anyone—do you hear?"

"As soon as we get home from school, we'll help you with the work, Mum, so we can get through early tonight," Mary volunteered.

"Got your boxing gloves ready for tonight, Nanna?" John teased.

"I think I'm past most of my good punches now, John, but Lorna is second to none when she gets wound up," the elderly lady replied. "My best years for the Society are past."

At last the great moment arrived, and it found everybody seated, ready for the study. Bob had been placed at the head of the table, and Lorna and Nanna toward the other end, with the rest of the family spread on either side except for John and Paul, who chose to sit on the arms of two old lounge chairs near the table. "This is spectators' gallery," John explained.

Bob offered a short prayer for guidance, and before anyone could utter a word, Lorna leaned forward to take charge. Tonight was vital; she must not risk losing this opportunity.

Although Lorna's confidence in the Watchtower had been shaken, she felt sure that the Witnesses are still Jehovah's special people and that no other organization could possibly be right.

Also she knew Christ had done away with the Ten Commandments. She felt that once she proved this point all the other Adventist teachings would collapse, and once again the truth of the teachings of the Watchtower would be vindicated.

"Bob," she began, "tonight we are going to study about these Ten Commandments of yours, which you maintain were written on tables of stone and placed in the ark. Is that right?"

"Yes," agreed Bob, "that is perfectly correct."

"And you also told Clarice that there was another division in the law, which was written in a book and placed in the side of the ark. Do you still stand by that statement?"

"I most certainly do."

"Well," Lorna said, feeling an almost motherly pity, "I'm afraid you are terribly mistaken, for nowhere in the Bible—Nanna and I have searched it thoroughly for a fortnight—will you find anything taken into the ark other than Noah's family of eight people, plus the animals, birds, and food!"

Clarice began to laugh, and Bob opened his mouth to say something, when Lorna cut him off.

"Now wait a minute, young fellow, this is my turn tonight. You have accused the Watchtower of teaching doctrines not supported by the Bible, but here is one of your Adventist ideas, and I've never heard anything more ridiculous."

"But, Mum," Clarice interrupted.

"Mum, nothing, my dear. This is. Bob's problem, and he has to get himself out of it."

"With the bricks!" added Gary.

Bob was about to speak again when Paul wanted to know what "bricks" had to do with it.

"It's just one of John's jokes," Lorna explained. "When we first heard about the tables of stone being put in the ark, John called them 'stones in the boat,' and then it came to 'bricks in the boat.'"

"I'm sorry to disappoint you all tonight," said Bob, "but there never were any 'bricks in the boat.' The stones were in a box instead. However, the box was an ark, known as the 'ark of the covenant.' Remember, there are two arks mentioned in the Bible."

"Ow!" sighed Gary.

"I guess we should have suspected something like this," Nanna said with disgust.

"The way Clarice described the tables of stone being 'taken and placed securely in the ark,' I had the mental picture of Noah tying them down," Lorna explained, "so they would not break as the ark pitched and rolled in the storm. And when she said the book was 'in the side of the ark,' I thought it would be kept safe in this way from the rats and goats that might have eaten it."

"That's a beauty, Paul!" said John, slapping him on the back. "That's one to tell your grandchildren!"

"I still want to see from the Bible," continued Lorna, "where Jehovah ever had two divisions like this in His great law covenant. Furthermore, if one division finished when Christ died, but the other remains for all to keep, then I want to see it proved from both the Old and New Testaments."

Bob took a chart out of his bag and hung it on the wall. He then placed on the table a slab of polished stone representing the Ten Commandments, and a small parchment scroll inscribed "The Law of Moses."

"What are they getting at?" Paul whispered to John.

"The Witnesses do not believe in keeping the Ten Commandments today, but the Adventists do."

Paul nodded in assent, as Bob began: "Well now, we'll open our Bibles to Deuteronomy, chapter 5. We will find in this chapter that the Ten Commandments were a separate law which was written on tables of stone by Jehovah."

"Do you mind using the New World Bible tonight?" Lorna asked. "I feel it is more modern, and a superior translation."

"If you would prefer it," Bob agreed. "But one of these days I'll show you some things about that translation that I fear will alter your opinion of it. However, we'll use it tonight."

He continued: "In verses 7 to 21 you will find the list of the Ten Commandments. Now someone please read verse 22."

"These Words Jehovah spoke to all YOUR congregation in the mountain out of the middle of the fire, the cloud and the thick gloom, with a loud voice, and he added nothing; after which he wrote them upon two tablets of stone and gave me them." Lorna paused as she glanced back over the text, and read to herself, *'And added nothing.'"*

"These were called the tables, or as you have it in your Bible, the 'tablets' of the Testimony," said Bob. "Now let's read Exodus 31:18 in the New World translation: 'Now as soon as he had finished speaking with him on Mount Sinai he proceeded to give Moses two tablets of the Testimony, tablets of stone written on by God's finger.' Now in Exodus 40:20 we read that this Testimony, in other words, the Ten Commandments, was placed in the ark."

Valmai read the text: "'After that he took the Testimony and put it into the Ark and placed the poles on the Ark and put the cover above upon the Ark.'"

"The other law," Bob explained, "was written not by God, but by Moses, who wrote it in a book, then put it in or at the side of the ark, separate from the Commandments inside the ark. You'll read about it in Deuteronomy 31:24 to 26."

"This sounds interesting," said Lorna. "Please let me read it. 'And it came about that as soon as Moses had finished writing the words of this law in a book until their completion, Moses began to command the Levites, the carriers of the ark of Jehovah's covenant, saying: "Taking this book of the law, You must place it at the side of the ark of the covenant of Jehovah YOUR God, and it must serve as a witness there against you."'"

A short silence followed, then Lorna said with a sigh, "Well, you are never too old to learn, and I'll grant you, Bob, that you've got something there. But in the New Testament it is all one law, which Paul vehemently worked to get rid of, because Christ had abolished it."

"In the New Testament Paul emphasized that no one could earn salvation by keeping law," Bob replied. "Repeatedly he taught that the only way a person could be saved and made righteous was by faith in the shed blood of Christ. But, so people would not go to the other extreme as many do today and conclude that there is no law for Christians to keep, he also contends that true faith, rather than doing away with law, establishes it in the life of the believer. Romans 3:31 is one of the many references of this nature." When all had found this verse, he read, "'Do we, then, abolish law by means of our faith? Never may that happen! On the contrary, we establish law.'"

"I still don't understand," Lorna said, shaking her head, "for in Romans 10:4 Paul tells us that Christ is the end of law, and to me that means it is all finished."

"I know that text well," Bob agreed. "In the King James it says, 'Christ is the end of the law for righteousness to every-one that believeth.' 'End' *(telos)* as used in this text means 'goal' or 'objective.' The two words 'for righteousness' give us the key to this verse, and it is just what I have been trying to say. Keeping any law will never make you righteous, and Paul always opposed this idea as a false method of salvation. On the other hand, we need to remember that he still preserved the law as a standard of revelation of God's holy character and will. This is why he says in Romans 7 that the law is holy, just, and good, and even tells us that it is spiritual. Spiritual people delight to keep a spiritual law, but Christ is their only righteousness."

"This does not mean any specific set of commandments, Bob. It is covered if we love God and our neighbor," Lorna suggested.

"I agree," said Bob, "that love should always be the motivating force behind our obedience, but we still need specific commandments as a definition of God's will, or we in our ignorance can err. In Romans 7 Paul says that he did not even know it was wrong to covet until he was confronted with the commandment that forbids coveting."

"How, then, do you know this includes all the Ten Commandments, and not the laws dealing with sacrifices and ceremonies, which Moses also gave?"

"This is where we need further understanding, Mum. In the New Testament we find that something is done away with, but also that something remains established. In the transition from the Old Testament to the New, you'll find that it is the blood sacrifices and ceremonies of the law of Moses that were discontinued, but the Ten Commandment law that remains, Otherwise you would have a terrible contradiction in the New Testament.

"In Galatians 5:2 and 3, we read that there is a law one should not keep; otherwise he has departed from Christ. Listen to this passage: 'See! I, Paul, am telling YOU that if YOU become circumcised, Christ will be of no benefit to YOU. Moreover, I bear witness again to every man getting circumcised that he is under obligation to perform the whole Law.'"

"Now we come to James 2:10 to 12: 'For whoever observes all the Law but makes a false step in one point, he has become an offender against them all. For he who said: "You must not commit adultery," said also: "You must not murder." If, now, you do not commit adultery but you do murder, you have become a transgressor of law. Keep on speaking in such a way and keep on doing in such a way as those do who are going to be judged by the law of a free people.'"

"So there you have it—a *whole* law which contains circumcision and such ceremonies, which is not to be kept. And we have *another* law which contains moral commandments forbidding adultery and murder, which we desire to keep in every point out of a heart of love, and we are going to be judged by it. As the Bible says, 'judged by the law of a free people.' It is the truth that makes us free, and it is the truth that reveals to us the Ten Commandments as an expression of God's eternal moral law.

"In Acts 15:5 the law which commands circumcision is called the law of Moses. I'll read it to you: 'Yet, some of those of the sect of the Pharisees that had believed rose up from their seats and said: "It is necessary to circumcise them and charge them to observe the law of Moses."'"

"So you would say, then," said Lorna, "that circumcision and other parts of the law of Moses are no longer necessary, but the keeping of the Commandments is?"

"That's exactly what Paul conveys in I Corinthians 7:19: 'Circumcision does not mean a thing, and uncircumcision means not a thing, but observance of God's commandments [does].'

"When you understand this truth on the subject of law in the New Testament, there are no more contradictions. Everything fits into place as the truth of God should. But remember, we keep these commandments because we love

The COMMANDMENTS of GOD

The Moral Law

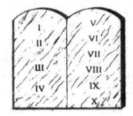

Before Sin
Defines Sin

MORAL lAW
(Ten Commandments)

1. Spoken by God . . . . Deut. 4:12
2. Written by God . . . . Ex. 31:18, Deut. 10:3,4
3. On Stone . . . . Ex. 31:18, Deut. 10:3,4
4. Kept inside Ark . . . . Deut. 10:1–5
5. Complete . . . . Deut. 5:22
6. Eternal . . . . Ps. 111:7,8
7. Holy, Just and Good. . . . . Rom. 7:12
8. Points out Sin . . . . . . 1 John 3:4, Rom. 7:7
9. Must not break. . . . . Matt. 5:19
10. Spiritual . . . . Rom. 7:19
11. Perfect . . . . Ps 19:7
12. Law of Liberty . . . . James 2:11
13. Delight. . . . . Ps 119:77,17
14. Christ magnified. . . . . Isa. 42:21
15. Till heaven and Earth pass . . . . . Matt. 5:18
16. Standard in judgment. . . . . James 2:12
17. A "WHOLE" law which **is to be kept** by Christians . . . . .James 2:10–12

The LAW of MOSES

The Ceremonial Law

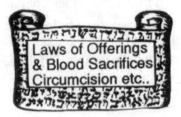

Laws of Offerings & Blood Sacrifices Circumcision etc..

After Sin
Defines Remedies

CEREMONIAL lAWS

1 Spoken by Moses . . . . .Lev. 1:1–3
2 Written by Moses . . . . .Deut. 31:9
3 In a Book . . . . .Deut. 31:24
4 Kept outside of Ark . . . . .Deut. 31:26
5. Added to and built up . . . Lev. 1:1–3, 4:1–3
6. Temporary . . . . .Heb. 7:12
7 Contrary, not good . . . . .Col. 2:14
8. Points to Saviour. . . Lev. 4:27–31, Jn. 1:29
9 Must not keep . . . . .Acts 15:24
10. Carnal .Heb. 7:16
11. Made nothing perfect. . . . . .Heb. 7:19
12. Yoke of bondage . . . . .Gal. 5:1
13. A burden . . . . .Acts 15:10
14. Christ abolished . . . . .Eph. 2:15
15. Till seed come . . . . .Gal. 3:19
16. Not used for judgment . . . . . . Col. 2:16, 17
17. A "WHOLE" law which is **not to be kept** by Christians . . . . .Gal. 5:1–3

the Lord, not because we have to or feel it will earn our salvation. When we fully accept Christ as our personal Saviour from sin, then we desire to stop sinning, and this means we bring our new lives in Christ into harmony with the commandments."

"When did the Adventists discover this?" Nanna asked.

"They didn't. The Reformers taught it centuries ago. In England, in 1562, the Anglican Church produced the 'Book of Common Prayer.' The seventh article reads: 'Although the Law given from God by Moses, as touching Ceremonies and Rites, do not bind Christian men, ...no Christian man whatsoever is free from the obedience of the Commandments which are called Moral.' In 1771 John Wesley on pages 339 and 340 of his book, *Fifty-three Sermons*, outlined the aspects of law, as being 'ceremonial,' the Law of Moses, and 'moral,' which he believed were contained in the Ten Commandments. The Presbyterian Church, in its *Shorter Catechism*, also teaches that man's duty is to keep the 'moral' law, 'summarily comprehended in the Ten Commandments.'"

"Well, the fact that Christendom has taught them for centuries does not impress me," Lorna said.

"Don't worry about Christendom teaching the Ten Commandments, Mum," said Bob. "They have taught them, it is true, but few of them have kept all of them."

"I don't care who teaches them, or keeps them!" protested Nanna. "Despite all you've said in defense of the Ten Commandments, I know that the Bible teaches the Commandments finished at the torture stake with the death of Christ Jesus."

"You'll never find a reference for that in the Bible," Bob insisted.

"Oh, yes we will!" said Lorna. "Our book, *Let God Be True*, has an excellent chapter on it, because if we have to keep the Ten Commandments, then we would also have to keep the weekly Seventh-day Sabbath. Since every statement in this book is supported with Bible proof, I know it will be here." She turned to the chapter entitled, "The Sabbath: In Shadow and Reality."

"You'll only find there what the Watchtower teaches, not what the Bible says," Bob cautioned. "You'll find references to where circumcision, and the laws dealing with the blood sacrifices of animals, were done away with at Calvary, and symbolically nailed to the cross, or torture stake. But there is no reference in all the Bible to say the Ten Commandments finished at the cross. Christians should keep the Commandments."

However, nothing could deter Lorna. She carefully scanned each paragraph for a clear-cut statement that the commandments had been done away at the cross.

At last she found what she had been looking for. "Here it is," she announced excitedly, and began to read: "Since God has taken the Jewish law covenant with its Ten Commandments out of the way by nailing it to the tree on which Jesus died, the Christians must observe, not the law—covenant shadows, but the reality." (Page 164, 1946 ed.)

"Now give him the Bible reference for it, Lorna!" urged John.

"There's none here, Dad," said Clarice, who had just read the statement in her own copy of the book.

"There's not, just here," Lorna admitted, scanning the page. "But, wait a moment and I'll find one here somewhere."

Lorna searched the next chapter of the book too. She saw texts which showed that the law of Moses was done away. She saw that the Watchtower had endeavored to get rid of the Ten Commandments along with it. But there was still no text to show that the commandments had been done away.

Usually she could give a clear Bible text for every statement she made, and she knew that all the family felt proud of her Bible knowledge. Now she felt she had failed them, and, more than that, fear began to grip her that perhaps what she had been taught all these years was wrong. She decided that the wisest plan would be to change the subject slightly and take the offensive again:

"Why are you Seventh-day Adventists so worried about the commandments? Is it because you keep Sabbath, but don't realize that the seventh day, like the other days of creation, is a period of 7,000? Don't you know that we are still living in this period?"

"I'm afraid that is another Watchtower teaching without Bible support!" replied Bob.

"But I just read it in *Let God Be True*, and I'm sure it gave Bible proof."

As Lorna reached for her copy of the book, Clarice and Bob took up their copies. Mary and Valmai moved to either side of Clarice to look on her copy, while Bob shared his with John and Paul, who by now were taking great interest in the proceedings.

Together they read the first few pages of the chapter "The Sabbath: In Shadow and Reality." In the second paragraph they read, "Measured by the length of the 'seventh day,' on which God desists from work and is refreshed, each of those days was 7,000 years long." Then they looked for a Bible reference to prove this, but Bob proved to be right again: there was no such text.

"Honey, I don't think it's here," said John to his wife.

"I've been let down again," admitted Lorna sadly, and burst into tears.

"I'm finished," she wailed, and picking up the book she had been reading, she hurled it across the room against the wall. "I'm finished forever, with religion and the lot!"

Nanna sprang to her feet. "Don't do that, my dear. I know the anguish you're going through. Seems as if all we've believed and cherished is crumbling at our feet, but there is an answer somewhere."

"Honey," said John, his voice sympathetic, "from what I've seen, it isn't God or the Bible that has deceived you—it's the Watchtower!"

Lorna shook her head in disbelief, and began to dry her eyes.

7

Answered Prayer

For two days Lorna refused to be consoled. She would not pick up a Bible or a book. She felt almost as if there had been a death in the family. She noticed that the other family members seemed to avoid mentioning the subject of religion, but tried to carry on normally as if nothing had happened. Then on the third day she went back to her books and Bible.

"So you've not given it up after all, honey?" John said, noticing the change with a smile.

"I just can't leave them alone any longer," she replied.

"I'm glad. You know, Lorna, you just can't live without religion. Why not relax and let it all sort itself out?"

"How do you relax when your salvation is at stake, and the rest of the family's? I'm the spiritual leader of this home, you know."

Previously Lorna had not prayed very much. She had joined in the prayer offered in the Society meetings, but prayer had never been a personal thing to her. However, as she read in Luke's gospel that Christ knelt down and prayed to His Father in the hour of His crisis, she realized how much more she needed help in her own crisis. That Thursday night she spent hours in prayer, asking for guidance to make the right decision. Should she keep the commandments or not?

The next morning when the children had left, Lorna sat at the breakfast table with her books as John read the morning newspaper. Suddenly, with her hand on her Bible, she prayed a short, desperate prayer: "Lord, help me find the truth!" Then she opened her Bible at random and began to read where it opened, in Roman 8: "Because the minding of the flesh means enmity with God, for it is not under subjection to the law of God, nor, in fact, can it be. So that those who are in harmony with the flesh cannot please God. However YOU are in harmony, not with the flesh, but with the spirit, if God's spirit truly dwells in YOU.

Suddenly she felt a thrill of joy. It seemed as if a light shone on the page. "John, I've got it! I've got it! You know how I've been worried about the Ten Commandment law, and why the Witnesses cannot see this truth? Well, listen to this!" And she read the verses aloud.

"This is talking about the change that comes into a person's life by the Holy Spirit. Jesus said it was being 'born again.' In order to be saved, a person must experience this change from the carnal, or fleshly, to the spiritual. That is what the Bible means when it says, 'Flesh and blood cannot inherit God's kingdom.'"

"Furthermore, the verse says that if a person has not had this change, then he doesn't want to keep the law of God, nor indeed can he. We Witnesses have been taught that only the 144,000 class need to be born again. I can see how it fits together, and I have my answer!"

John breathed a sigh; it sounded like a sigh of relief. "I hope the struggle's over soon," he said.

"Nanna's not up yet, but I must go and show Clarice what I have discovered," she said impatiently. Leaving the dishes on the table, she hurried out of the house.

When Lorna reached Clarice's home, she found that everyone had gone out. But she entered the house, found Clarice's Bible, and opened it to Romans, chapter eight. She wrote a note to tell Clarice to read it.

On her return, she found that Nanna was up and dressed, so she hastened to share her discovery with her, only to receive a real disappointment. By the time she had finished discussing it with Nanna, she found herself confused again.

Early that afternoon, Lorna heard a knocking at the door. It was Bob. Immediately Lorna began to tell of her immediate answer to prayer. "What do you think of it?" she asked.

"I'm not at all amazed," Bob replied. "This sort of thing does not happen very often, but I know of other cases where the Lord has dramatically answered sincere prayer. God is not dead, you know!"

"But what is in that chapter, anyway?" asked Nanna.

"It's the answer to your problems, as Jehovah's Witnesses seeking salvation," he replied. "When Jesus said to

Nicodemus, 'Ye must be born again,' He stated a truth that applies to every soul that is to be saved. If the Holy Spirit does His work in our lives, we will be born again. If He does not, then, irrespective of who we are, we will be lost. Now, if you are born again, then you have a heavenly hope, for all the saved have a heavenly hope."

"Oh, no, they don't," Nanna contradicted. "That would mean the great multitude would enter heaven."

"That's exactly what the Bible teaches, Nanna. In Revelation 7:9 You will find this company so numerous that no one can number it in heaven. They are standing before the throne."

"They could still be standing before the throne and be on the earth," Nanna countered. "The earth is His footstool."

"The Bible leaves us in no doubt as to what it means," Bob explained, "for in Revelation 19:1, King James, it says, 'And after these things I heard a great voice of *much people in heaven*, saying, Alleluia; Salvation, and glory, and honor, and power, unto the Lord our God.' This 'much people' is from the same word in the Greek translated 'great multitude' in Revelation 7:9."

"But you have read from the King James Version? What about the New World Bible?"

"I'm afraid it is no help to you, Nanna," Bob replied. "In fact it clarifies the case by using 'great crowd' in both places and identifying this 'great crowd' of Revelation 7:9 which cannot be numbered, with the 'great crowd' which is 'in heaven.'"

"But doesn't it say in Revelation 19:1 that it is 'the loud voice in heaven of a great crowd?'" Nanna persisted. "It is the voice, not the crowd, that is in heaven!"

"No, it doesn't. You read it for us, please," replied Bob.

Nanna found the place and read, "'After these things I heard what was as a loud voice of a great crowd in heaven.'"

"They are up there all right, Mother," Lorna said, but the old lady remained tight-lipped and offered no comment.

"Do you believe then that those mentioned in the Old Testament could go to heaven too?" Lorna felt a little bewildered. "The Watchtower is emphatic that no one who lived before Christ died will ever go to heaven!"

"Elijah is already there. The Bible, in Second Kings 2:11, tells how he was taken up into heaven by a whirlwind. Also Enoch—the Bible says he 'was translated that he should not see death.'"

"Where does it say that?" Nanna questioned.

"In Hebrews 11:5."

"I must check that up in my Bible again."

"Read what it says then, Mother," her daughter suggested.

The old lady took a quick glance at the text and answered, "You can, if you like."

Lorna picked up her Bible and read; 'By faith Enoch was transferred so as not to see death, and he was nowhere to be found because God had transferred him; for before his transference he had the witness that he had pleased God well.' If he did not die and he was transferred off the earth, it is pretty obvious he must be in heaven, I suppose."

"That's right!" Bob agreed. "While we are in this chapter, look at some of these other verses about Abraham, Isaac, and Jacob having a heavenly hope. In verses 9 and 10 we read: 'By faith he [Abraham] ... dwelt in tents with Isaac and Jacob, the heirs with him of the very same promise. For he was awaiting the city having real foundations, the builder and creator of which [city] is God.'"

"If they were awaiting a city built by God Himself, then they'd have wanted something better than Beth-Sarim!" Lorna observed, smiling.

The old lady did not look amused. "And where is this city of God, in heaven or on the earth?"

"I'll read you your answer from your own Bible, Nanna," said Bob obligingly. "It's found just over the page in Hebrews 12:22, 'But You have approached a Mount Zion and a city of [the] living God, heavenly Jerusalem, and myriads of angels.' There is your answer, Nanna. It's the 'heavenly Jerusalem,' and the angels dwell there too."

"And in what form will they go there?" asked Nanna, with an air of unbelief.

"This time we'll read Philippians 3:20 and 21: 'As for us, our citizenship exists in the heavens, from which place also we are eagerly waiting for a savior, the Lord Jesus Christ, who will refashion our humiliated body to be conformed to his glorious body according to the operation of the power that he has, even to subject all things to himself.' There it is; Christ will return from heaven with a body, and He will change, or refashion, our bodies. Remember, they are not spirits; they have bodies, just like Christ's body."

"Wasn't the resurrected Jesus a spirit, who has gone to heaven that way?" was Nanna's next question.

"No. Let's read Luke 24:37 to 39: 'But because they were terrified, and had become frightened, they were imagining they beheld a spirit. So he said to them: "Why are You troubled, and why is it doubts come up in your hearts? See my hands and my feet, that it is I myself; feel me and see, because a spirit does not have flesh and bones just as YOU behold that I have.'" Isn't that plain?"

"But I think the body Christ assumed when He appeared to His disciples, so they would not be frightened of Him, would have been laid aside before He reached heaven, possibly dissolved into a gas, so that He would have entered into His Father's presence as a spirit."

"In the *Emphatic Diaglott*," said Bob, "the translators describe this entrance of Christ as being in the flesh! Do you have a copy there? The reference is found in Hebrews 10:20."

Lorna opened the text and read, "Which Way he consecrated for us, through the VAIL (that is, his FLESH, recently killed and yet is living).' Fancy that!" she added, "the word 'flesh' is in capital letters! This would mean that Christ Jesus is a Man in heaven, then?"

"He's more than that, of course, but he does retain His humanity," he explained. "In First Timothy 2:5 the Bible describes His work in heaven in these words: 'There is one God, and one mediator between God and men, a man Christ Jesus.'"

"So you believe that when He returns He will be the same Person as the One who left on the day of His ascension?" asked Nanna.

"From these texts," interrupted Lorna, "the Bible teaches that Christ had a body. He was resurrected and went to heaven with a body, in which He will return—a perfect, glorious body. Then He is going to change our bodies to be like His; then we are ready to go to heaven with Him."

"I'm afraid I can't believe that!" objected Nanna. "It's all right if you can, but all I want to do is to stay on the earth and not have to keep those commandments!"

"Well, Nanna," said Bob seriously, "I hope and pray the day will soon come when you will want to go to heaven and you will find joy in keeping the commandments."

He looked at his watch. Time was passing, so he offered a short prayer and bade them goodbye until the following Monday night.

When Bob left, Lorna felt a real peace in her mind, but it was short-lived. As they prepared their evening meal, Nanna thought up every problem and objection she had learned in her years in the Society.

8
A Debate

By the following Sunday morning, Nanna had arranged for the congregation servant and his wife to pay her a visit. Lorna liked this couple very much. They were about the same age as she, and over the years they had become good friends. When Ron and Joan Roberts arrived, Lorna greeted them with pleasure.

"We cannot stay long," they explained. "We just thought we'd drop in and see how you've been."

"I'm glad you've come," said Lorna, "because there is a young Adventist minister who has been calling, and he is getting me a bit confused."

"Such as?" Ron inquired.

"Well, I think the thing I'm worried about most is whether we should keep the Ten Commandments or not."

"Oh, don't worry about that," he answered. "A couple of texts and we'll fix him. When does he call?"

"Tomorrow night."

"We'll see you then if that's all right."

"Ron's never lost a debate yet," Joan assured her, "so you'll have something to look forward to tomorrow night." They made a few comments about the farm and the weather and then drove off to their next appointment.

Lorna went up to the milking shed and told John of the arrangements. "Are you going to warn Bob?" he asked.

"I don't think so," Lorna reasoned. "If he has the truth, then he should not need any warning."

That afternoon John saw Norm and Betty Anderson, the Adventist couple, and told them of the arrangements made for the next night. "Poor Lorna doesn't know what to believe," he said. "One day Bob has her convinced the Adventists are right; then Nanna goes at her with Watchtower arguments. I think she really believes you Adventists are right, but her loyalties are still with the Watchtower

Society. Tomorrow night should settle it with Ron Roberts matched against young Bob!"

When Bob arrived at "Blue Gums" Monday night, he noticed a couple of extra chairs placed in the room. "Are we going to have visitors tonight?" he asked pleasantly. No one answered him at once, and the conversation centered on lines of farm activity and the damage the kangaroos were doing to the pastures.

Then they heard the sound of a car coming up the driveway.

"I've asked Ron and Joan Roberts to come out tonight," Lorna explained simply, and went outside to meet them.

Bob met the guests and then excused himself to go out to his car. John and Lorna guessed he wanted to spend a few moments in prayer.

When Bob returned to his place, Lorna brought the group to attention. "I've brought Ron and Joan out tonight to defend me." She looked at Bob.

"What do you want to study?" Ron Roberts asked.

"The law!" Lorna pounded the table for emphasis. "I want that settled once and for all!"

"Since it is really Bob's study," suggested Ron, "he had better speak first."

Bob reached over and selected the book *Enemies* from the bookcase where Lorna kept her Watchtower publications. "I believe we should keep the Ten Commandments, and agree exactly with what the Watchtower teaches on page 94 Of this book. And since I could not express it more clearly myself, I'll read it to you:

"'Therefore God gave his law through Moses to the Israelites and which applies to all who want to do right, and the first in order and first in importance of his commandments or fundamental law is this, to wit.' It then goes on to quote Exodus 20:1–6," he explained, "which is the first part of the Ten Commandment law. But listen to what follows: 'The law of God never changes, because God never changes. (Malachi 3:6). His law points out the way to everlasting life. No creature will ever be given life everlasting who willfully, that is, intentionally, violates God's law....For a man to violate the fundamental law of God means that that man puts himself on the side of the devil, who therefore leads him to destruction.'"

"So there it is!" Bob announced. "It is a very serious thing intentionally to break these commandments."

Ron Roberts was a heavyset man with a reddish face and hair that had turned prematurely white. However, by the time Bob had finished reading from his own Watchtower publications, Ron's face was crimson, and his wife shuffled uneasily by his side.

"That's an old book!" he said with disgust. "We don't teach that anymore. That book was published back in 1937."

"If it was taught as truth then," Bob questioned, "why should it be error now?"

"Because we have greater truth now, and we know that the Ten Commandments were done away with at the torture stake."

The young man looked the older squarely in the eye and asked, "Tell me, Mr. Roberts, what does the Watchtower have against the Ten Commandments? Would you want to have another god before Jehovah, bow down to images, or take His name in vain?"

"No!

Bob left out the fourth commandment and proceeded with the others. "Is it that you do not want to honor your parents, or you want to kill, commit adultery, steal, bear false witness, or covet ?"

"No. We agree with all that."

"Well, where is the trouble?" Bob questioned.

"It's that Sabbath!" the older man exclaimed.

"So, to get rid of the Sabbath you want to destroy this whole law, as Herod slew the children attempting to destroy Christ?"

"No," the older man countered, "it's just that it was only given to the Jews, and when Christ died it finished. Now we are not under law but under grace. Similarly, there was no law before God wrote the commandments on tables of stone and gave them to Moses."

"I think we had better test these statements by the Bible," Bob suggested meekly.

"This is what I want," said Lorna, "the case for and the case against."

"First," Bob continued, "we'll look up Romans 5:12 to 14, and we'll find that Paul states there was law from Adam to Moses. He argues it this way: He says that there was death during that time, and that was the result of sin. But if there was sin, then there must have been a law to break!"

They read the passage, and everybody nodded agreement.

"However," the older man argued, "this law was not the commandments. It certainly did not contain the Sabbath."

"I'm afraid you will be proved wrong again," Bob said. "Let's look at Exodus 16, where we read of Israel being fed with manna before they reached Sinai. We will read verse 4.

"In what Bible?" questioned Nanna.

"I prefer the King James Version, because the New World translation was printed by the Watchtower with its distinct viewpoints. However, we will use the New World Bible if you prefer it," Bob conceded.

Nanna seized the opportunity and began to read: "'Then Jehovah said to Moses: "Here I am raining down bread for YOU from the heavens; and the people must go out and pick up each his amount day for day, in order that I may put them to the test as to whether they will walk in my law or not"'"

"There we have the fact of a law before Sinai, where the commandments were written on the tables of stone," Bob affirmed. "Now we will find that one of the commandments in this law was the keeping of the Seventh-day Sabbath."

"You remember that they were to gather so much manna each day; then on the sixth day they were to gather twice as much, for none would be given on the Sabbath. However, the very Sabbath after they were told about the manna, some disobeyed and went out looking for it. God was displeased with their disobedience. We'll read about it in verses 27 and 28."

Lorna put her reading spectacles back on and read, "'However, it came about on the seventh day that some of the people did go out to pick [it] up, but they found none.

Consequently Jehovah said to Moses: "How long must YOU people refuse to keep my commandments and my laws?"'"

"There it is!" Bob declared, "There is no mistake here that Jehovah considered the Sabbath commandment as part of His law. It is interesting to note that this must have been known for a long time, for Jehovah asks the question of them, 'How long?'"

"Well, this is the time of Moses," said the congregation servant. "Perhaps we could allow that, but if there was a law, then it was not known earlier."

"Yes, it was!" Bob replied. "Someone please read Genesis 26:5."

Clarice obliged. "'Due to the fact that Abraham listened to my voice and continued to keep his obligations to me, my commands, my statutes, and my laws.'"

"So God had Abraham keeping 'my laws.' Then as we read in Exodus 16:4, He tested them in relationship to keeping the Seventh-day Sabbath, a part of 'my law.'"

"Well, that clears that up for me," Lorna decided.

"Of course Abraham was the father of the Jews, so I guess we could expect that. The Sabbath was given to the Jews, but to them exclusively; it was never intended for the Gentiles!" Mr. Roberts countered.

Bob then suggested that they turn to Isaiah 56, where he began to read verse 2. "'Happy is the mortal man that does this, and the son of mankind that lays hold of it, keeping the Sabbath in order not to profane it, and keeping his hand in order not to do any kind of badness.' It is interesting," he observed, "that Jehovah says a man who keeps the Sabbath is happy. Then He says this privilege is also extended to the Gentile or foreigner who joined himself to Jehovah. Perhaps Nanna would like to read this in verse 6."

Despite her years, Nanna's voice came through clear and strong: "'And the foreigners that have joined themselves to Jehovah to minister to him and to love the name of Jehovah, in order to become servants to him, all those keeping the Sabbath in order not to profane it and laying hold of my covenant.'"

"Thank you, Nanna," said Bob.

"But this is the Old Testament," the older man protested.

"You said the Sabbath was never for the Gentiles, Mr. Roberts, and I have shown you that it was. Now I'll show you the same thing in the New Testament. First we will read Acts 17:2 and 4: 'So according to Paul's custom he went inside to them, and for three Sabbaths he reasoned with them from the Scriptures.' 'As a result some of them became believers and associated themselves with Paul and Silas, and a great multitude of the Greeks who worshiped [God] and not a few of the principal women did so.' There you have the Gentiles, a whole multitude of them. Here is another reference in Acts 18:4: 'However, he would give a talk in the synagogue every Sabbath and would persuade Jews and Greeks.' And verse 11: 'So he stayed set there a year and six months, teaching among them the word of God.' It all adds up to the Sabbath being kept by both Jew and Gentile, Mr. Roberts, don't you think?"

"Not at all! I do not think Paul had any respect for the day at all. He just found he could regularly get a convenient congregation in the synagogue on a Sabbath, so he went there."

"I'm afraid this argument is going to crumble too," Bob said confidently. "When we read Acts 16:13, 'And on the Sabbath day we went forth outside the gate beside a river, where we were thinking there was a place of prayer; and we sat down and began speaking to the women that, had assembled.'"

"Now, notice first, there is no synagogue in this place—Philippi, a Roman colony—but Luke, the Bible writer, many years after Christ's death calls this day 'the Sabbath day.' We find Paul specially going out of the bustle of the city to this quiet place of prayer beside a river, because it was the Sabbath."

"That's pretty plain, isn't it, Mum?" Gary observed.

Lorna did not want to hurt Ron's and Joan's feelings, so she chose not to answer him. An awkward silence followed, until the congregation servant decided to speak again.

"This weekly Sabbath idea was just a hangover from the Jewish traditions, but as the Christians realized the truth of the real Sabbath period Of 7,000 years, they realized they had to keep every day for the Lord, not just one day in seven."

Bob disagreed. "The Bible does not teach the Sabbath was a period of 7,000 years or any other day of creation."

"But surely you know, Bob," the older man persisted, "that a 'day' can be more than twenty-four hours. Many times 'day' refers to long periods of time."

"Yes, I know. But whenever a day has a numeral in front of it, such as 'first' day, or 'second' day, it never means any period other than a twenty-four hour day. In the concordance are scores of references to 'day' but never an exception to this. When Genesis 1 speaks of the evening and the morning as the 'first day,' it clearly means a twenty-four hour day.

"If the days were 7,000 years long, they comprised an evening and a morning, then you would have 3,500 years of light and 3,500 years of darkness. Vegetation could not have grown this way after it was created. Furthermore, with vegetation created the third day, then it would not have been pollinated by the bees and insects for many thousands of years. But more than that, the Bible says God spoke everything into existence, and it would not take the Almighty thousands of years to do that."

"But," the Witness leader broke in, "what Jehovah did speak into existence had to grow and mature, so everything would be in readiness for man to be put on the earth. That would take much longer than twenty-four hours!"

"No, Mr. Roberts," Bob replied, "when Adam was created, he was a mature man, not a baby to grow up. Similarly, all the other creation was mature too. The grass was spoken into existence yielding seed, the trees yielding their fruit."

"Ron," asked Lorna, "can you find a text in the Bible to say that each day of creation was 7,000 years long? That's what I tried to find last week and could not."

"It does not exactly say 7,000 years," Ron hesitated. "But it does say that a day is a thousand years, and the seven days of creation would add up to 7,000 years."

"Hey, there," put in John. "That's not right; each day has to be 7,000 years long itself, and the week adds up to 49,000 years. That's what I read in *Let God Be True*."

"Yes, John, I know." Ron blushed slightly. "But then, this is just the principle of reckoning that I was referring to, with emphasis on the fact of the day being the long period of time—not so much the sum of the actual figure."

"Mr. Roberts," said Bob, "you claimed that 'a day is a thousand years,' but this is a misquotation of Scripture. Read Second Peter 3:8, and you will find you have left out the word *as*, and this prevents the text from being used as a time rule."

Determined not to be beaten, the congregation servant brought up another argument: "The fact that the Sabbath is a period of 7,000 years is also proved from Hebrews 4:9, where it says, 'So there remains a Sabbath resting for the people of God.'"

"If you examine that text in the Greek and in its context," replied Bob, "rather than proving the Sabbath is a 7,000-year period, it proves that the people of God should still be keeping the Sabbath."

"We'll look it up in our *Emphatic Diaglott*, Ron," Lorna suggested. "If we get it straight from the Greek, that will settle it for us."

They found the passage and carefully read each interlinear English word under the Greek text: "'Therefore remains a keeping of a Sabbath for the people of God.'"

"There's no doubt about the fact we should be keeping a Sabbath," said Lorna. "Just depends upon what kind it should be."

"That is no problem," said Bob. "If you look closely at the word for 'keeping of a Sabbath' you will find it is *sabbatismos*, which means Sabbath rest or Sabbath observance. That is why people who keep the Sabbath are said to *sabbatize*."

"I can see that plainly enough," Lorna observed.

"Mum, look at this," said Clarice suddenly. "In verse 4. 'For in one place he has said of the seventh day as follows: "And God rested on the seventh day from all his works."' Here it does not say He is 'resting,' as if He has been resting 7,000 years, but it is something finished, in past tense: 'God rested.' Also note, this refers to the Seventh-day Sabbath."

"Look, though, in verse 10," Valmai added. "'For the man that has entered into [God's] rest has also himself rested from his own works, just as God did from his own.' Here is the past tense again: 'God did.' It links up with verse 9, that this Sabbath to be kept is the seventh day: 'Just as God did from his own' refers back to verse four, which names 'the seventh day.'"

"If you read on the next verse," Bob added with a smile, "it will leave you in no doubt whatsoever, that it is the Seventh-day Sabbath of the commandments. It mentions 'disobedience,' and the Seventh-day Sabbath is the only one we have ever been commanded to obey."

Valmai read on, "'Let us therefore do our utmost to enter into that rest, for fear anyone should fall in the same pattern of disobedience.'"

"Summing these verses up," Bob explained, "the writer of Hebrews tells us that many of the Israelites did not reach Canaan because of their disobedience and lack of faith. Similarly there is danger for Christians, that they will not finally be saved in the kingdom of God because of their disobedience and lack of faith. Isn't it rather curious that Hebrews specially links this up with the keeping of the Seventh-day Sabbath, the one all Christendom, including the Witnesses, trample on?"

"Please don't link us with Christendom," Ron protested.

"There are many wonderful people in the churches throughout Christendom, as there are many sincere people among the Jehovah's Witnesses, who believe they are pleasing God. Yet they ignore a test of religion Jesus summed up when He said, 'If ye love Me, keep My commandments.'"

"It is only the Sabbath commandment we don't keep," Ron protested. "We keep all the others."

"Mark 2:28 says that Christ claimed to be Lord also of the Sabbath, and what we need here and now is to accept Him and love Him with all our hearts. Then we will also love and respect His special day. I do trust that this will be the experience of all here tonight," Bob smiled.

"Well, I think we had better go now," said the congregation servant, looking at his watch. "It is amazing how time gets away when you are deeply engrossed in the Bible."

Lorna went out with them to see them off. They shook her hand and said, "We're sorry, Lorna, we could not do better for you tonight. We have never met anything like this before in all our years in the Society!"

Many thoughts coursed through Lorna's mind that night. "What do I do now?" she asked herself.

9

Decision

"I wonder what happened up at 'Blue Gums' last night," said Betty Anderson to her husband as they finished their morning chores. "I'm sure Bob has powerfully presented Bible truth, but Ron Roberts has a reputation of being a real Watchtower champion,"

"Well, I have to go up there this morning," said Norm. "I promised John the loan of my tractor and also told Lorna she could have some more tomatoes. Perhaps I'll hear something about the debate."

Norm drove the tractor the mile to the Stevenses' farm, stopping just outside their back door. John came out to meet him and offered to drive him back to his farm.

"That's all right, John," Norm said, "I can walk to save you the time. Besides, I want to check our boundary fences, for the kangaroos have been breaking them down lately."

"Since this dry weather, with little bush grass around, I don't think a six-foot fence would keep them off our pastures," John observed.

"Say, here is something I promised Lorna the other day." Norm picked up the bag of tomatoes.

"Bring them in and give them to her yourself," John replied. "Since I told you what had been planned for last night, you might as well come in and hear all about it." Norm followed John into the house.

"Nice to see you, Norm," Lorna greeted. "Take a seat."

Norm settled down in an easy chair.

"You should have been here last night," Lorna began. "You know we brought Ron Roberts up to straighten us out. I've never had any intentions of being anything but a Jehovah's Witness, and Bob had upset my thinking on a lot of things."

"Well, what happened?"

"Happened! I've never seen anything like it in all my life. I would never have believed it could happen to a congregation servant like Ron, if I had not witnessed it myself. Bob swept every Watchtower argument before him, and at times left Ron quite speechless!"

"It was really terrific, Norm," John agreed.

"In fact," Lorna continued, "right throughout the whole evening Ron couldn't give one point that Bob didn't prove wrong from the Bible."

"Young Bob's so clear in his presentation too," John added. "He gave Bible proof for every statement he made."

"What was the discussion all about?" Norm asked.

"The law," Lorna explained. "There are dozens of things I would like to have straightened out, but I thought that one was the most important. If we should keep the Ten Commandments, then it's pretty serious business to ignore them. With both sides represented, I wanted to see who taught the truth and who taught error."

"So you feel Bob had a convincing case?" Norm questioned.

"Convincing!" John exclaimed. "The most convincing thing I've ever heard."

"And it all came from the Bible," Lorna added. "Bob even used our Bible, which of course was not written to support the Ten Commandments and the Sabbath!"

"Well, now," asked Norm, "what are you going to do?"

For a moment Lorna remained silent. This was the problem she had been wrestling with all night, and she knew it called for a decision.

"Guess there is only one thing I can do and be honest with my convictions," Lorna replied. "I must accept Christ fully as my personal Saviour from sin, and stop sinning." Then she looked at Norm. "I know Jesus said 'If anyone wants to come after me, let him disown himself and pick up his torture stake and continually follow me.' But is it a terribly awful experience keeping the Sabbath?" she asked.

"Not at all," laughed Norm. "Remember, Jesus also said, 'My yoke is kindly and My load is light.' You will find after you have kept a few Sabbaths that you will wonder however you got on without the blessing it affords each week."

"But, whatever do you do?" she questioned further. "Do you have to stay in bed all day, or sit around and do nothing? In all the years I have been in the Society, I have always thought that nothing worse could happen to a person than to keep a Sabbath each week."

"We really enjoy the Sabbath; it is a day of special fellowship with Christ. We look forward to it each week," her neighbor assured her. "If you accept Christ fully, you will greatly enjoy it too!"

"Would you make your decision for Christ with me, John?" Lorna asked her husband.

John hesitated. Then he declared, "Honey, I'll be with you!"

Lorna's eyes flushed with tears of joy.

"What about the rest of the family and Nanna?" Norm asked.

"The family seem enthusiastic enough," Lorna replied. "Except Nanna. She was pretty silent last night when she went to bed. I don't think she is happy about things at all, but that will make no difference to me once I have made up my mind."

"Do you have a church, Norm?" John asked.

"Yes! Would you like to come this Sabbath?"

"Well, Bob read to us last night about Paul going to a place of worship each Sabbath. So I guess if we are going to do the thing properly, we had better start doing likewise," Lorna reasoned.

"I'm thrilled," said Norm. "Since Betty and I moved into the district four years ago, we have prayed earnestly for you. We directed Bob first to Clarice, and that's how all of this started."

"Norm," Lorna queried, "when Betty has been here on a Friday, I've heard her say she had to get home early to 'prepare for Sabbath.' What did she mean?"

"In the Bible, Friday is called the 'preparation' day. You'll read about it in Luke 23:54–56. However, I'll tell you what— I'll bring Betty over tonight, and we'll tell you all about our church services. Also, we'll bring you a lesson pamphlet which we study each week, and Betty can explain how she prepares her cooking and the house on Friday so the Sabbath is free to enjoy. It's the best, most enjoyable day of the whole week in our home."

"That would be wonderful," Lorna replied. "We do have tonight free, but I have to leave for the city soon to do some shopping today, so I hope you will excuse me." Lorna slipped away to get dressed for town, and the men returned to the tractor.

When Lorna arrived in the city, she parked her car on the main thoroughfare, and had no sooner locked it up, than who should she meet but Joan Roberts.

"Hello, Joan," she greeted. "How are you this morning?"

"Don't ask me, Lorna. You know it was midnight when we got home last night. We were so upset that we decided to study out what Bob said, and we never went to bed until five o'clock this morning—and then we couldn't sleep!"

"John and I stayed awake a long time last night ourselves before we dropped off," Lorna confessed. "He certainly gave us something to think about."

"You know, Lorna," the other woman added, "if what that young chap says is right, then we are wrong! It has really 'rocked' Ron."

"Do you think Ron would ever budge from the Society?" Lorna asked. She thought of the years he had defended its teachings and the persecution he had suffered for it, particularly during World War II.

"I doubt it," came the reply. "Besides, we just could not imagine any organization being right other than the Watchtower, despite anything anyone could show us."

"Well, if a thing is wrong we must leave it, and if it is right we must accept it," Lorna affirmed. "Loyalty to the Watchtower is not going to save any of us."

Lorna spent no more time in the city than necessary. On her return, she talked with Nanna of her decision. However, Nanna said she was far from happy about it. "Even if you have lost faith in the Watchtower, you don't need to join the Adventist Church," she told her daughter. "And as for me, my loyalties are still with the Society."

When the Andersen arrived that evening, Nanna politely retired to bed, not wishing to discuss religion with them.

By the end of the evening, which they all thoroughly enjoyed, Lorna decided she would look forward to her first Sabbath and attending church. She also thought that the idea of studying a weekly Sabbath School lesson was a wonderful way to encourage daily Bible study.

When Clarice learned of her parents' decision, she was thrilled. "Mum," she said, "I knew it was the truth from the first time Bob called on me. It all seemed so logical and simple; and more than that, it was straight from the Bible, not from books like the Watchtower studies. But I never ever thought you would change."

"Nor did I," said her mother with a smile; "but there is still Nanna to battle with, and of course I must tell David and Brenda. We shall have to work for them now."

"Of course, Mum. But we still don't know everything about the Adventists, do we?"

"No, but I'm not worried about the tiny details. I'm confident they will all fall into place. All the big things are right, and the more I check them the more clear they become."

Clarice could not wait to tell Paul the news when he came in that night. While he was pleased they were leaving the Witnesses, he said he wished they would join a more "respectable" church than the Seventh-day Adventist. When she told him she was considering going to church with her parents next Sabbath, he curtly informed her that, while he would not stop her going to church, he would not agree to her taking the children.

Bob Watson had had no contact with "Blue Gums" since the Monday evening, so he was oblivious to what had been happening. Norm and Betty Anderson, thinking it would all be a pleasant surprise for him, decided to leave it that way.

So it was that as Bob sat in Sabbath School that Sabbath morning, he was amazed to see Norm and Betty Anderson lead John, Lorna, Valmai, Mary, and Gary, followed by Clarice, to a seat. After the service, as the congregation gathered in the porch of the little country church, Lorna pushed through the crowd to greet Bob. "Here we are," she announced smilingly. "You told us if we were honest we would be Seventh-day Adventists!"

She shook his hand with deep feeling. "You know, since I made my decision this week, I have known a tremendous peace in my soul that I have never experienced before. Everything is fitting together perfectly, and I am wonderfully happy."

John stood by her side, but seemed a little too choked for words, which would have been superfluous anyway.

"Where is Nanna?" Bob asked with obvious concern.

"She would not come. She is intensely loyal to the Watchtower, and all her friends are in the Society too," Lorna explained. "But deep in her heart she knows this is right, and we believe she will soon join us. Mother, too, has always been honest with God."

Norm and Betty Anderson invited the Stevens family to their farm for lunch. Since Clarice had to get home to Paul and her children, she arranged to pick Nanna up and take her home to her place for lunch. The old lady thought the world of Clarice and enjoyed a few hours with her great-grandchildren.

As they drove along, Clarice told Nanna what a wonderful time they had had at church that morning, and asked, "What did you do, Nanna?"

"Well, if I tell you the whole story, my dear, promise not to tell your mother. You know how pushing your mother is, and I don't want to be pushed into anything."

"I'll keep it to myself," Clarice promised.

"Well, I went to start some sewing, but somehow I just could not sew. Then I went to finish off some knitting, and once again I could not do it. Something kept saying, 'This is the Sabbath of Jehovah your God.' I got quite annoyed, and felt very rebellious, but it was not until I picked up my Bible and began to read that I got any peace."

"Nanna, you're going to be with us, I can see," said Clarice. "This reminds me of the text that says something like this, 'Your own ears will hear a word behind you saying: "This is the way. Walk in it."'"

"Well, it says walk, not run, and since I'm pretty slow at walking these days, I'm not to be hurried. Also, I still have lots of questions on other things the Adventists teach."

Over on the Andersen' farm, Lorna joined Betty in her kitchen as she readied lunch. Lorna was amazed to find such an attractive meal all cooked and prepared the day before. Conversation at the table never lagged, for there was much to talk about. Then there were questions, so many questions they wanted answered at once!

It was late in the afternoon when they tore themselves away from the Andersen.' When the evening shadows were beginning to creep, and the last rays of the sun dropped behind the western hills, they thanked God for their first happy Sabbath. This was a foretaste, they felt, of heaven itself, but an experience unknown in the teachings of the Watchtower.

10
Paradise Restored

At the study the next Monday night, Lorna asked Bob to outline all the events connected with the 1,000 years of the "millennium."

"I know you went through it briefly when you called one day," Lorna said, "but now everyone is here, and I would like you to outline it again."

Bob took a roll of charts from his satchel and reviewed the fact that according to the Bible the *parousia* of Christ is "near," but still future. Then he showed a chart which pictured Christ in the clouds of heaven surrounded by angels. In one corner the destruction of the wicked and Armageddon was depicted, and in the other a scene of the resurrection. An angel stood at the open graveside, as all the resurrected were about to be "caught up in the clouds to meet the Lord in the air."

"There are only two classes when Christ returns," Bob summarized. "Those who will be saved and those who will be lost. The Bible speaks of them as the 'sheep' and 'goats,' 'wheat' and 'tares,' 'wise' and 'foolish'—one class is saved, the other lost.

"In the parable of the wheat and the tares, the wheat was all gathered into the one barn, and the tares burned. In John 14:1 to 3 Christ says when He returns He will take His people to His Father's house, so we know that the saved will be taken to heaven."

"Why could that not apply to just the 144,000, Bob?" Nanna queried.

"Because of the context of the chapter, for one thing," Bob replied. "Verse 15 says that those that love Him should keep His commandments, and then He would give to them the Comforter, which is the Spirit of truth, or the Holy Spirit.

"We know that the Holy Spirit is not limited to the 144,000, nor is the obligation to keep the commandments.

Similarly, the heavenly hope is not limited to 144,000, but to all who receive the Holy Spirit and are saved."

"That adds up with what I discovered from Romans 8," said Lorna. "Those who are led by the Spirit are changed from carnal to spiritual, or 'born again.' These people then want to keep God's law, and that chapter shows that they have a 'heavenly' hope. Reading a 144,000 into these chapters is a Watchtower teaching, but not implied in the Bible."

"Now we come to those who are to be saved," Bob continued. "When Christ returns, some are alive on the earth and others asleep in death. First Thessalonians 4:13 to 17 describes how Christ descends from heaven announced by trumpets, and the 'dead in Christ' are resurrected first. These are caught up in the clouds with those who are already alive, to meet the Lord in the air. All will thus be forever with the Lord."

"Surely those living on the earth already are not taken to heaven as they are?" asked John.

"No," said Bob, "those who are alive when Christ returns are changed in a moment, in the twinkling of an eye, when the trumpet sounds. We will read about it in First Corinthians 15:51 to 54." They all read the passage together.

"There are also those who are lost," Bob continued. "First of all, the wicked dead are not raised, for the Bible says at that time only the 'dead in Christ' are resurrected. Then Second Thessalonians 2:8 tells us that the wicked are destroyed by the brightness of His coming or *parousia*. Luke 17:26 to 30 and Matthew 24:38 and 39 liken this destruction of the wicked to that of the Flood, and also to the sudden destruction of Sodom in the days of Lot."

"Who is left on the earth, then, if all the saved are in heaven and the wicked are dead?" John asked with keen interest.

"Must be no one," concluded Gary.

"Right!" Bob agreed. "A Bible description of an empty earth is given in Jeremiah 4:23 to 27. The cities and the fruitful places have been broken down at the presence of the

| Armageddon Christ Comes 1st Resurrection | Earth Desolate Thousand Years Satan Bound | City Descends 2nd Resurrection Wicked Destroyed | Earth Renewed God's Throne on it Paradise Restored |

Lord and by His fierce anger. The whole land is *desolate*. However, the Bible adds that God will not leave it that way."

Using both the New World and the King James versions of the Bible, the group continued to examine the passages.

"What happens to these people on the earth?" came another question.

"They remain like rubbish on the face of the earth, *from one end of the earth to the other*," he replied. "In the language of Jeremiah 25:33, they will not be lamented, gathered, or buried."

"So we'll not have to bury those bones for seven months after all!" said Clarice with great relief. "I've always dreaded the thought of that after Armageddon."

"You certainly won't," Bob agreed. "The Bible says there is no one even to bewail them, let alone gather or bury them." Bob explained. "In Revelation 20, we will check what we have read in those passages in Jeremiah and Ezekiel. The first few verses tell of an angel coming down from heaven to the earth, which is in a chaotic condition—an abyss or 'bottomless pit.' Here the devil is bound so he cannot deceive the nations for 1,000 years, for there is no one alive for him to tempt. But at the end of that time he will be loosed for a short time.

"Jeremiah described the earth when there was no one to deceive, and earlier tonight we studied from the New Testament how this came about: The saved are in heaven, and the wicked are dead. So in this solitary prison Satan is bound, with no one to tempt."

"During this time, verse 4 gives us a picture of the saved in heaven with Christ. It specially mentions those who are martyred for their faith. Since there are millions who died during the Dark Ages for even the little truth they knew then, we know this number is many more than a mere 144,000, but would be the great multitude that no one can number, as well."

"Verse 6 tells us that the saved are resurrected in the first resurrection, and will not die in the second death. However, verse 5 mentions the wicked dead, who are not resurrected until the end of the 1,000 years."

"Let me read that verse again," said Lorna: "'The rest of the dead did not come to life until the thousand years were ended.' That's amazing, for in the last chapters of the *Paradise* book, the Watchtower teaches that these people are resurrected *during* the 1,000 years. The Bible clearly says that they do not come to life until the thousand years *are ended*! That's plain enough."

"If the wicked are resurrected at the end of the thousand years, what happens then?" asked John, anxious to get on with the series of events.

"Exactly what you would imagine. Satan goes to work again deceiving and leading a rebellion." Bob paused. "Let us read it from the Bible in verses 7 to 9."

"'Now as soon as the thousand years have been ended, Satan will be let loose out of his prison, and he will go out to mislead those nations in the four corners of the earth, Gog and Magog, to gather them together for the war. The number of these is as the sand of the sea. And they advanced over the breadth of the earth and encircled the camp of the holy ones and the beloved city. But fire came down out of heaven and devoured them.'"

"So here is Gog and Magog at last," Lorna observed. "Now I can see that Ezekiel 39 does not apply directly after Armageddon to Gog and Magog having their bones buried for seven months, because they are depicted here as the wicked 'like the sand of the sea' who are destroyed after the thousand years."

"Right," said Bob. "See how simple and clear the Bible is? This also helps us to understand how, by comparison, the great multitude is still 'a little flock.'"

"Where does this city come from?" Nanna put in. "How does it suddenly appear on this desolate earth with all the saved in it?"

"How do we know the saved are in it?" Clarice added.

"Because the Bible says this city is the 'camp of the saints' or the 'camp of the holy ones,' depending on your translation."

"Why camp? Is it some temporary home of theirs?"

"Yes," replied Bob. "But let me answer Nanna's question first. In Revelation 21, the first few verses tell us that this city comes down from God out of heaven. That is how we find it on the earth. Naturally when Satan sees this city, he reasons that he, with the wicked of all ages, could overthrow it. In his hatred of God and His people he goes up to do this.

"As these wicked people surround the city they see what they have missed because of their disobedience, and it is then they are given their final pronouncement of judgment. This is where 'all stand before the judgment seat of God' and when 'every knee' bows, and 'every tongue' confesses that Jesus Christ is Lord.

"Then it is that fire comes down from God out of heaven and devours them. To use the language of Malachi 4:1 to 3, the destruction leaves them neither root nor branch. They are consumed like stubble and become ashes. This is the death that we are saved from by Jesus' dying on the cross.

"This fire then cleanses the earth and the Lord brings it back to its Edenic beauty. The promises of Isaiah 65:21 to 25 are fulfilled as the saved build their own homes and inhabit them, and plant vineyards and eat the fruit of them.

"All that was lost in Eden will be restored, only this time the City of God will be on the earth. The throne of God and of the Lamb (Christ) will be here and, as Revelation 21:3 states, 'God Himself' will dwell with them."

"Seems unbelievable, about this city coming down from heaven and God dwelling with mankind," said Nanna.

"God knew that people would reason this way. This is why He instructed John the Revelator to add in verse 5: 'Write, because these words are faithful and true.' They are not a fairy tale or parable. All of this is true, and will happen faithfully as it has been described."

"I must sit down and read these last chapters of Revelation again," Lorna said. "What we have heard tonight is marvelous, and it is so clear and straight from the Bible."

"How can we be sure that this city is real?" asked Nanna.

"We have read our answer from the Bible," Bob replied. "Now we will look at this with our own powers of logic. Take the tree of life in the original garden of Eden—do you believe it was a real tree ?"

"Of course."

"Do you believe the tree of life in Paradise restored mentioned in Revelation, will be a real tree?"

"Yes, indeed."

"Do you believe it will grow on either side of a real river?"

"Yes, I guess so."

"Well, now, we have a real tree of life growing on either side of a real river, which flows from the real throne of God, which is in the midst of the city—how then could the city be anything but real? Jesus said, 'In my Father's house are many mansions, if it were not so I would have told you.' It is real, all of it."

"The more we learn this clear Bible truth, the more wonderful it all becomes," observed Lorna. "It makes me wonder why I did not understand it years ago."

"The trouble was, Lorna," said John, "once you heard of the Watchtower teachings, you would not look past them. Whenever you had anything pointed out to you from the Bible, you would only interpret it in the light of Watchtower teachings."

"What do you think of it all, Dad?" asked Clarice.

"It makes sense at last, Clarice," he answered. "For years I have felt that the Witnesses have had something, and for that reason I have come along with you to meetings and conventions. But I have never joined because I have always felt something was not quite right. There was too much of man's interpretation, and not enough Bible."

"If you are going to be an Adventist, John," Nanna said bluntly, "you will have to give up smoking!"

"If a thing is worth it, I'm happy to give up smoking for it," John answered, unruffled. "And when did you last see me smoke, Nanna? Let me tell you a secret: I have already given up smoking, and I believe Jesus Christ will give me the faith never to go back to it."

Lorna felt such a thrill that her eyes filled with tears. It was all wonderful, unbelievable. This was another answer to her prayers.

"This is the truth, and the power of the gospel," she said to herself, "a power I never knew in the teachings of the Watchtower."

11

One God or Two?

As Lorna Stevens looked up, she saw Clarice's car coming up the driveway and hurried out to meet her.

"Mum, have you heard the latest?" Clarice looked excited. "The Witnesses have told their people not to listen to Bob when he calls on them, as he is a deceiver, a wolf in sheep's clothing!"

"Oh, no! They would not do that!"

"Well, I know for a fact that they have. I met Bob in the town today, and he said the Witnesses will not open their doors to him. Later I met a couple of Witnesses, and they said the congregation servant told them not to look at a book of Bob's or let him read any part of the Bible to them. He also announced that he had met Bob here and had completely disproved every statement he made."

"I've never heard anything like this before," said Nanna indignantly. "In all the years I've been in the Society we've said that Jehovah's truth can stand up to any test. We've been happy to meet anyone. Tell Bob to go down and speak to David and Brenda before they are told to turn him from their doors!"

"Nanna!" said Lorna amazed. "Who are you batting for? I thought you were trying to keep us all in the Society."

"This is different." Nanna could hardly conceal her displeasure. "I've despised the ministers of Christendom for teaching their flocks to turn us from their doors, but I never thought I'd live to see the day when the Society would do this."

"Well, Bob has visited a lot of Witnesses in his door-to-door work, and a lot of them are losing confidence in the Watchtower," said Clarice. "His knowledge of the Watchtower history and teaching is devastating, as we have found out ourselves. Then, some of them saw us going to the Adventist church on Sabbath, and that has worried them still more."

"If they know we have started to go to the Adventist church since the debate, that indicates how thoroughly Ron Roberts answered the Adventist teachings!" Lorna said with a smile. "Anyhow, I agree with Nanna. We should not wait any longer to tell David and Brenda what has happened. They should investigate it all and make up their own minds. If you go to the city, Clarice, could you see them?"

"I've been waiting for this opportunity," responded Clarice. "I'll go this very afternoon and tell them of our new faith."

When Bob called on David and Brenda two days later, he found David had just filled out his monthly report for the Society. Like his mother, he zealously put his hours in and placed a good quota of magazines. The two young men discovered they were about the same age, and soon were earnestly discussing the Trinity. Brenda looked on as she tended the baby.

"I believe there is only one solitary being from all eternity—Jehovah God, the Creator and Preserver of the universe and of all things," David explained to Bob. "Jesus Christ, I believe, is 'a god,' the 'beginning of the creation of Jehovah and the only-begotten of the Father.' The Holy Spirit is an active force, certainly not a person."

"You know, David," Bob began. "I understand how you have come to these conclusions, for I too have studied Watchtower books deeply—Let *God Be True* and others. But this teaching is neither logical or Scriptural. It contradicts what the Watchtower is endeavoring to teach!"

"How do you make that out?" David asked, astonishment written on his face.

"First of all, the Watchtower emphasizes that there is only one God, and I agree with this statement. But when we examine the Watchtower teaching, we find two Gods, not just one after all. There is Jehovah God, the Father, who is the Almighty God; then in the New World translation of Isaiah 9:6 we find it prophesied that Jesus is to be a 'Mighty God.' So there is an 'Almighty God' and a 'Mighty God.'"

"Now this is where Watchtower teaching conflicts with the Bible on this subject, for Isaiah 43:10 says no God was formed either before or after God, and He certainly could not be a second God. The Watchtower teaching is far more confusing than anything it claims about Christendom's views on the Trinity.

"If we could deny the deity of Christ entirely, as the Watchtower has tried to do, it might simplify matters. But Scripture teaches that Christ is divine—He is God. Let us look at Matthew 1:23; John 20:28; Philippians 2:6 to 11; I Timothy 3:16; Titus 3:4; and Hebrews 1:8. We simply cannot deny the deity of Christ, in view of clear Bible texts."

"Then you believe that Christ and His Father died together on the cross, and were both baptized in the river Jordan by John?" asked David.

"Not at all, David. You and Brenda as a married couple are as 'one,' yet you are two different persons. Likewise, the Father and Son are both divine, but they are two separate Persons, although they belong to the one Godhead."

"Do you believe the Holy Spirit is a person and part of this Godhead, too?" David asked.

"Definitely," said Bob. "Let us look up Romans 8. Your mother could tell you some interesting things about this chapter."

"So I believe," David agreed. "I'm really interested to examine this chapter now, but do you mind if I use my New World translation ?"

"Not at all," said Bob, "but I must remind you that if there was one reason more than another why the Watchtower produced the New World Bible, it was not to uphold the deity of Christ or the Trinity. However, the truth is still in the very translation they have produced, as you will see in our study together. We will read verse 34 of Romans 8, and use that translation too!"

"'Who is he that will condemn? Christ Jesus is the one who died, yes, rather the one who was raised up from the dead, who is on the right hand of God, who also *pleads* for us.'"

"Do you believe, David, that one could plead for us if he was not a person?" Bob asked.

"Of course not," David agreed, "but what has this to do with the Holy Spirit?"

"In this verse it says, 'who also pleads for us.' Already this chapter mentioned another Person who pleads for us, so Christ Jesus is mentioned as 'also' pleading. Verse 26 says this Person is the Holy Spirit: 'In like manner the spirit also joins in with help for our weakness; for the [problem of] what we should pray for as we need to we do not know, but the spirit itself pleads for us with groanings unuttered.'"

David reread the passages and remarked, "Fancy that! I've never seen it before."

"Here is another text to mark, which proves the Holy Spirit is a Person: Ephesians 4:30. It says that a person can 'grieve' the Holy Spirit. You cannot grieve a force, you can only grieve someone with feeling and the attributes of personality.

"Look at John 16:13, where Jesus said the Holy Spirit would guide into truth and teach. He would speak, but not of Himself. Then Acts 13:2, where the Holy Ghost calls Himself 'me.' These are just a few references."

"That is a good start anyway," David agreed. "Can you show me that the Holy Spirit is spoken of as a being 'God?'"

"Yes, in Acts 5:3 and 4 Peter accuses Ananias of lying to the Holy Spirit, explaining that this is lying to 'God.'"

"Now that you have established that the Holy Spirit is a Person," David continued, "does the Bible include these three Persons in the Godhead that you have mentioned?"

"It mentions that the Holy Spirit is inseparably joined to the Father and the Son by a singular common name, in the same way that a married couple have one family name. It is in this name that people are to be baptized. Let us look at Matthew 28:19, where it says 'name,' not 'names,' of the Father, Son, and Holy Spirit."

"That's interesting," observed David. "I have often wondered how and why there was just one name mentioned in this text. But now, wouldn't we have three Gods? Wouldn't this make matters worse than the two you say the Watchtower has?" He was frankly puzzled.

"No," Bob smiled. "This is where the confusion arises concerning the Trinity. Each person is not 'a' God; it is the three persons that are God, or make up the 'Godhead.' It is like having a government, which is a singular word but made up of a number of members. No single member is the government, but all go to make up that government as individual members.

"In the Old Testament the Hebrew word for God is 'Elohim,' which is plural, meaning more than one person. When we read texts like Matthew 28:19 and 2 Corinthians 13:14, we understand the deeper significance of this fact."

"Is there an example in the Old Testament," asked David, obviously intrigued, "where more than one person is mentioned in connection with 'Elohim?'"

"Yes, in Genesis 1:26: 'And God went on to say: "Let us make man in our image, according to our likeness."' 'So at creation 'God' was more than one person. It seems significant that this truth should be introduced in the very first chapter of the Bible."

"I can follow you as far as you have gone," agreed David, "but I still have a lot of questions. What do you believe is the divine name—is it Jehovah?"

"We cannot be sure," Bob replied. "The Watchtower has made much about that pronunciation, but all we can be sure of is the four consonants YHWH. The vowels have to be supplied, which means the name may have been pronounced any of several ways. However, if the pronunciation of the name were important, would not Christ have told us, and left no one in doubt about it?"

"Do you feel the name is not important, then?" David queried.

"The name is important, but let us remember that the important part is not the sound of the name, but what it stands for. A person's name may be Jones, Brown, or Smith—it matters little. But what it stands for and who it represents makes all the difference. With God, it is not the exact pronunciation of His name, but His nature, authority, dominion, and government. We must never be sidetracked over the name of God, while living out of harmony with all that name stands for."

"Perhaps this is why we do not know the exact name of God," David suggested.

"Yes," added Bob, "and even if we could be sure about the exact name, I don't think I'd be using it a great deal. In British countries we know that the name of the Queen of England is 'Elizabeth,' but we usually speak of her as the 'Queen' or 'Her Majesty.' Unless we are identifying which sovereign she is, to use her name is not necessary or in the best taste. The same, of course, applies in a family. A son who continually refers to his father by his given name is considered disrespectful. With God, our Sovereign and our Father, we as His subjects and children should use His name sparingly and with care and respect."

"You're right," David agreed. "In the future I don't think I'll be using the name 'Jehovah' quite so frequently. Now my next question centers around two texts: Revelation 3:14 and Colossians 1:15. Do these not prove that Christ was created? He was the 'beginning of the creation by God,' and the 'first-born of all creation.' You do not believe this, though the Bible says it so clearly. Now tell me why."

"There is no problem with either text," explained Bob. "Revelation 3:14 says Christ is 'the beginning of the creation by God, not the first thing created, but rather the One responsible for beginning the creation of God. You know how the mayor first suggested, then planned and raised funds to build the new hospital? Today Tom Marsh is referred to as the 'beginning' of the new hospital—he began it. He was not the first stone laid, nor the first patient in it; he was the person responsible for it. So it is with Christ, the Creator."

"Christ, the Creator?" David questioned.

"Yes, in John 1:3 and Colossians 1:16 and 17 the Bible emphasizes that everything created was created by Christ. Nothing has been created, which was not created by Him. This rules out the idea that He was a created being.

"Now let's look at Colossians 1:15, which says Christ is the 'first-born' of all creation. Actually this passage explains itself. 'First-born' does not mean brought forth or created first, but it means *the One who is preeminent*, as expressed in verse eighteen. In other Bible passages we also find this so—Psalm 89:27, for example."

Both young men turned to the passage in their Bibles.

"This passage," Bob continued, "states that God was going to make of David a 'first-born' higher than the kings of the earth. But God was neither David's literal father, nor was David the eldest son. Rather, he was the youngest of many sons. 'First-born' meant he would be preeminent, over all other kings.

"Also, in Jeremiah 31:9, Ephraim is said to be 'first-born,' though Reuben was Jacob's real first-born, as recorded in Genesis 46:8. In Exodus 4:22 Israel is called 'my first-born.'

"Finally, the fact of 'first-born' not meaning 'brought forth first,' or 'created first,' but rather 'preeminent,' is made clear and definite in verse 18 of Colossians 1, It says He is the 'first-born from the dead, that he might become the one who is first in all things.' Christ is the one who has broken the shackles of the tomb, and all who are resurrected depend on Him although in the point of time Christ was not the first person to be resurrected."

David also carefully checked these references, then observed, "You mentioned that you believe Christ was the Creator. Is this one of the teachings of Seventh-day Adventists?"

"Definitely. The Bible leaves us in no doubt about this. John 1:3, Colossians 1:16 and 17, and Hebrews 1:2 affirm that God created all things by Jesus Christ.

"Since we know from Hebrews 11:3, Psalm 33:6 and 9, and Genesis 1 that everything was spoken into existence, it was Christ who did this work, and He did it for His Father. When it speaks of Him as God, we understand the Bible speaks of God the Son. In Genesis 1:26 we find that God the Father and God the Son considered the creation of man together. Then it was God the Son who created man."

"Later I'll study with you about the Seventh-day Sabbath. I'll show you that since Christ, or God the Son, was the Creator who actually did the work of creating on the six days, then it was Christ who rested from this work and instituted the Sabbath. This is why it is the 'Christian Sabbath,' and why Christ claimed it was His day. He is 'Lord also of the Sabbath.'"

"We'll have to leave it here today, Bob," David said. "I have to be at work soon. You have given me plenty to 'chew' over, but I'm afraid I could never accept what you have been saying today. I think I'll need a lot of convincing."

12
Who Is Jehovah?

When Bob called the next week, he found David ready with new questions. "Bob," Dave began, "during the week I began to wonder about what you have told me. Do you consider Christ also to be called 'Jehovah?'"

"Definitely!" said Bob. "Since the Father, Son, and Holy Spirit have the one 'name' (Matthew 28:19), that would be so just as your name is Stevens, so also is your wife's and your son's name. You, Brenda, and the baby can all claim the name of 'Stevens' as a family unit or individually. You can say 'My name is Stevens' or 'My family name is Stevens.'"

"I understand how my name is 'Stevens,' and it also applies to the three of us. But Jehovah would never speak of His name and apply it to 'Us,'" David contended.

"Jehovah does just that," said Bob. "Look at Genesis 3:22, and we'll read from your Bible too. Remember, 'God' is this plural 'Elohim' we mentioned last week. 'And Jehovah God went on to say: "Here the man has become like one of us."'"

"Well," declared David, "I've never seen that before."

"Here is another reference—Genesis 11:6 and 7: 'After that, Jehovah said:…"Come now! Let *us* go down."'"

"Now then," said David, trying to remember all he had learned, "this means Christ could claim the name 'Jehovah' as well as the Father, and I suppose the Holy Spirit too."

"That's right. In the Old Testament the Holy Spirit is called the 'Spirit of Jehovah,' and is mentioned in connection with men like Gideon, Samson, Elijah, Saul, Zechariah, and others. David prayed that the 'Holy Spirit' would not be taken from him.

"As for Christ Jesus, when He came to earth to die as our Saviour, He was named 'Jesus,' meaning 'Jehovah is Saviour.' As *Let God Be True* points out at the beginning of the third chapter, 'The name *Jesus* or *Jeshua* is just the shortened form of the Hebrew name *Jehóshua*, meaning *Jehovah is the Saviour.*'"

"Let us now compare these Old Testament references to Jehovah, and we will find them applied to Jesus Christ in the New Testament. Compare Isaiah 44:6 with Revelation 1:8 and 17; 2:8; 22:12 and 13—'First and the Last.' Compare Deuteronomy 32:3, 4 and 18 with 1 Corinthians 10:4—the 'Rock.' Compare Isaiah 40:3 with Matthew 3:3—'the way of Jehovah.' See Psalms 45:6; 102:24 to 27 and Hebrews 1:8 and 10 to 12—God's throne and everlasting life are applied to Christ. Compare Isaiah 6:1 to 3 with John 12:41—the 'glory' of Jehovah. Notice Ecclesiastes 12:14 and 2 Corinthians 5:10 and John 5:22—the 'judge.' Both Exodus 20:10 (first part) and Mark 2:28 speak of the 'Sabbath' of Jehovah. There are many others."

David compared each verse in both versions of the Bible, and also those in the New Testament with the *Emphatic Diaglott*. When he compared Hebrews 1:8 in the New World Bible and the *Emphatic Diaglott*, he remarked, "You said that the Watchtower had 'obscured' the meaning of many texts, this one has been almost 'mutilated.' In fact, I first noticed it last week when we were studying the deity of Christ. The King James version reads, 'But unto the Son he saith, Thy throne, O God is for ever and ever.' The *Emphatic Diaglott* has it, 'But to the son, "Thy Throne, O God is for the age."' However, the New World puts it, 'But with reference to the son: "God is your throne forever."' Seems ridiculous for God to be a throne!"

"If you knew Greek and Hebrew, you would be still more displeased with the way the New World translation deals with this verse and with others," Bob declared. "When there is a particular Watchtower teaching they want to uphold, it is amazing what they do to Scripture in that translation. But fortunately there is usually a verse or two that escapes their attention. Then there is a real contradiction."

"That's what Mum said the other night," David said. "Can you give me some examples? I'm going to ask them about it when I go to the next meeting of the Society."

"Sure," said Bob. "We are a little sidetracked, but perhaps it would be a good thing for you to know about our studies. I used mostly the New World Bible with your people, when they decided the Watchtower did not teach the truth. So it does not depend entirely on which version you use. But one thing is certain: the New World translation is by no means a translation of superior accuracy."

"Now, in our study so far, we learned that everything created was created by Christ. But, since the Watchtower teaches that Christ Himself was a created Being, you will see in Colossians 1:16 and 17 that the Watchtower has supplied the word *other* four times to infer that Christ was created first; then He in turn created all the other things. Check this with the *Emphatic Diaglott* and you will find the word *other* is not in the Greek text."

"This makes the Bible contradict itself, because in John 1:3 they forgot to supply the word 'other.' It reads, 'All things came into existence through him, and apart from him not even one thing came into existence. What has come into existence...'"

"I'll give you another example: Turn to Genesis 1 and 2, and you will find the tense used in the days of creation has been changed from the past tense to a continuous tense. Instead of reading 'God said' it reads 'God proceeded to say.' This is to give the impression each day was not an ordinary day, but a long period of time. When they come to the seventh day, in Genesis 2:1 to 3, instead of 'God rested the seventh day' they have it that God 'proceeded to rest on the seventh day.' Also, 'he has been resting,' so that if the seventh day is 7,000 years long, then God is still resting and we are still in that Sabbath. When you come to the New Testament, in Hebrews 4:4 and 10 they have forgotten to alter the tense. Although it is a quotation from Genesis 2:3, it reads, 'God rested on the seventh day.' In verse 10, speaking of God having rested from His works it says, 'just as God did.' So you have the contradiction of whether God is still resting, or whether God did rest the seventh day!"

David made a careful note of these texts.

"I must ask about all this at our next Society meeting, for we are told that the New World translation is more accurate than other translations, especially the King James," David said. "The unfortunate thing is that I do not know Greek or Hebrew, and neither does anyone else in the congregation. Maybe that's why we believe it is a superior translation. I still have faith, though, that the mature brothers of our Society can answer my questions."

13

Questions!

Several weeks later, Bob met David again. "How have you been?" Bob greeted him.

"I've had a rough time," David admitted. "I've asked lots of questions at our Society meetings, and most of them they can't answer except to say I should be studying Watchtower books more. Some of the mature brothers of the congregation avoid me, as they don't like my questions. No one seems able to explain why the Watchtower teaches everyone will be resurrected by the end of the thousand years, while Revelation 20:5 clearly states that the 'rest of the dead' will not live again until the thousand years are ended."

"I asked why Isaiah 66:22 and 23 mentions the keeping of a Sabbath each week in the New World, when they oppose keeping the Sabbath now?"

"They also find Enoch a problem, since Hebrews 11:5 says he has been transferred by God, and that he has not seen death. Yet he is not on the earth today, and the Watchtower teaches that no one before the time of Christ can go to heaven. When I ask these and many other questions from the Bible, and questions about the history and teachings of the Watchtower, I find myself increasingly unwelcome. They call me one who 'causes divisions,' although this is far from my intention."

"Now, Bob, I am faced with a real problem. I don't want to become a Seventh-day Adventist, and it would be hard for me if I did want to. My job sometime involves the Saturday day shift. I have worked up to the rank of foreman and make twice as much pay as a day worker."

"There's something else too. When I joined the Witnesses, television had just been introduced here and my baptism was televised. It seemed as if all the thousand employees of the factory saw me baptized, and how they did take on about it! Now, if I should admit I was wrong, will they ever laugh and jeer!"

Bob visited David and Brenda as often as he was able, and on one of these visits David told him, "I'm determined, if I find truth in the Adventist Church, to follow it. But I've just had my faith shattered in one organization, and I wonder if I will have enough faith to join another."

Brenda soon became more convinced than David that the Adventists are right, so when he eventually made his decision to attend an Adventist church, she happily accompanied him. At first their church attendance was rather spasmodic, as David was determined not to rush into anything too quickly. Also, he had to work frequently on Sabbaths. The church they chose to attend was not the large one nearby, but the little country church where the rest of David's family attended. By this time, Nanna also accompanied them, as did Clarice and her children. Paul, Clarice's husband, had decided that Adventists were not so "odd" after all, and he appreciated the change for good that had come into Clarice's life.

One Monday night, when David and Brenda had come up to "Blue Gums" to join in the regular study there, Lorna observed, "Sometimes I wish I had never been a Jehovah's Witness, for I have had to unlearn so much."

"I would not say that, Mum," said Bob. "The Watchtower teaches a great deal of truth. If it did not, it would not win so many honest souls like you. Many, when they discover some truth such as the unconscious sleep of the dead, find it such a revelation they assume everything else the Watchtower teaches is also truth."

"I can see now that they haven't got even that straight, teaching that people have been going to heaven in spirit form since 1918," she replied.

"At least, knowing that death is a sleep did help you eventually to sort out the truth," Bob consoled her.

"Then there were things which the Watchtower never even taught," she said.

"What are some of them?" David asked his mother.

"The wearing of pearls and other outward adornments," she replied.

"Where in the Bible does it tell about that?"

"In First Timothy 2:9 and 10 and First Peter 3: 1 to 4," she answered.

"What is your attitude toward Christmas, Bob?" David asked.

"Same as the Watchtower attitude toward Sunday," Bob replied. "We know that both days were dedicated to the sun god, worshiped by the ancient pagans. However, the Watchtower ignores the Sunday part of it and holds Sunday meetings because it is convenient to spread their teachings, since folk look on it as a day of religious meetings. Why not take the same consistent attitude toward Christmas?"

"Viewed in that light," Brenda observed, "the Watchtower is not very consistent, for it teaches us to have nothing to do with Christmas because of its pagan associations. Yet they make Sunday the day for their greatest religious activity and meetings."

"What about birthdays?"

"What about them?" Bob replied.

"Doesn't the Bible condemn celebrating them?" David asked.

"There is nothing in the Bible about it," Bob replied. "It does mention some pagans who celebrated their birthdays, but this does not make it wrong just because the pagans did it. The pagans had weddings also, but we will not stop getting married because they married. Naturally, a Christian would celebrate a wedding or birthday differently."

"What attitude should a Christian take to saluting a flag, and standing for a national anthem or ruler?" came the next question.

"These are tokens of loyalty and honor, and we are commanded by the Bible to be loyal and show respect. Romans 13:1 to 7 has a deal to say on this subject, and so does I Peter 2:13 to 18, which even says it is 'the will of God' for us to do this."

"Isn't this an act of worship?"

"Never," said Bob. "This is merely carrying out the command to render custom to whom custom is due, and honor to whom honor. An act of worship is entirely different.

If a king or high government official should visit an Adventist gathering, the congregation would stand or salute as a sign of respect. But if Jesus Christ came into their midst, the congregation would kneel to worship."

"That all makes sense to me," Paul remarked. "It is what I had always understood from my reading of the Bible as a young person."

"The whole teaching of the Adventist Church adds up to me," John added. "The more I hear, the more I am convinced that at last I have found what I have wanted for years. Now I am looking forward to being baptized an Adventist."

"Who else is planning that way, Mum?" David asked.

"There's your father and I, Valmai, and Mary. Gary is a little too young, though he says he wants to be baptized too. I don't know about Nanna, but Clarice would like to be baptized with us if Paul will agree."

"I would not stand in her way, only don't ask me to be baptized yet," Paul smiled.

"I know it is right," said Nanna, "but it's hard to make a sudden change at my age. I loved the Society. I know I must make the final break, and I plan to be in the baptism after this one."

"Now, David and Brenda," Lorna asked, "what about you two?"

"Well, we think it is the truth too, Mum," David replied. "But this time I am not going to take any risks. I want to study thoroughly into Adventist history and teachings. When I am absolutely sure, then I will face the problem of arranging my work to keep the Sabbath. It will mean I'll have to start as a new hand on day shift, and will only receive about half the wage, but I'm still prepared to do it."

Lorna felt a thrill of joy. This was better than her dreams, to have the prospect of her mother, husband, and all her children united in a faith that was becoming more wonderful and precious with every passing day.

Bob had prayed at the close of each study that they would be an unbroken family in the kingdom. Now Lorna could see the beginning of the answer to this prayer.

14

Baptized Into Christ

Winter had passed. The wattle trees, adorned in their golden mantles, heralded the Australian spring. An occasional kookaburra laughed with its mate in the gum trees, as the Stevens family drove their car along the familiar bush road that led to the little Adventist church.

This was a day they would never forget—the day when they would publicly accept Jesus Christ as their God and Saviour. Lorna's mind went back to that hot summer morning when Clarice had driven up to "Blue Gums" and announced that she intended to become a Seventh-day Adventist. So much had happened since then, but now she could see that the hand of the Lord had led them step by step into His truth. Over the months they had gained more than knowledge. They had gained a new experience and above all a personal Saviour from sin.

The little church that day seemed to have the blessing and atmosphere of heaven. The five candidates dressed in their neat baptismal robes, seated themselves at the side of the font, which had a mural and floral decorations to represent a river scene.

Sitting in one of the front pews were Brenda, David, and Paul, with Nanna between Gary and the children.

Bob preached the sermon, taking Galatians 3:27 as his text, "For as many of you as have been baptized into Christ have put on Christ." He explained the significance of baptism by immersion, and what it meant to be born again.

Betty Anderson sang a special consecration hymn, and while the organ softly played, John and Lorna led the way hand in hand into the waters of baptism.

For a moment a scene flashed back into Lorna's mind, of a hot, dusty afternoon years before. Then, in a borrowed dress, she had been baptized in an old bathtub at a convention held by the Witnesses on a race course. It seemed more unreal now than ever, and the contrast stood out in bold relief. Now, at last, she not only knew what it meant to be baptized into Christ, but she had experienced what it meant to "put on Christ."

After her baptism, Lorna visited through the district and told her neighbors what she had done. After having taught Watchtower beliefs for eighteen years, and having made converts to the Society, she did not find it easy to admit she had been wrong. However, Lorna went courageously forward to do what she now believed was her duty. She prayed that the Lord would not only give her strength to do her task, but that He would help her find souls to share the blessings of His truth.

When, at the end of the next year, Bob baptized twenty-three souls, among them were some Lorna had helped to win.

For months after the baptism, Bob still continued his studies with David and Brenda. David examined the history of the Adventist Church and their interpretation of prophecy. Out of months of study emerged the picture of an organization led by God, going steadily forward, with its truths becoming clearer and more beautiful with the passing years. On the other hand, he saw in the Watchtower a society wracked with changed doctrines, erroneous prophecies, and internal strife.

Among the books he read and enjoyed were those of Ellen G. White, particularly *The Great Controversy*. As he read this work written over seventy years before, with its detailed insight into the future, and compared it with the Watchtower publications of seventy years before, his mind held no doubts that Adventism is God's channel of truth for these last days.

Eventually the day came when he determined he would step forward and do what he now knew to be right. He told Brenda of his decision, and she happily assured him she would stand by him, whether it meant lower wages or any other trial. When David notified his manager that he intended to become a Seventh-day Adventist, and wanted Friday nights and Saturdays free, he was met with ridicule. Ministers and lay preachers of various churches were called in to talk him out of his "Sabbath nonsense," but David took his Bible to work and silenced each one in turn.

David had held a good position in the factory. He was such a reliable worker that his superior tried to arrange for him to have Sabbaths off. But this was against factory policy. Eventually his employers put him on day shift as a common factory hand, where he worked for lower wages along with the young workers who had just finished school.

Later on, as he looked back, he felt that perhaps the Lord had allowed him to experience these difficulties. He had always thought Jehovah's Witnesses were the only ones who suffered in any way for their faith. Now he knew different.

One day as he was working at home, three leading brothers of the Witness congregation, including the one that had studied with and baptized him, came to question him. They began to tell him that he was taking not only himself but also his little family to destruction.

David took the Bible he had marked during his studies with Bob, and began to ask questions of his visitors. "If you have the truth," he urged them, "answer my questions."

But they could not and left in disgust after warning that he would be disfellowshipped after being baptized into the Adventist Church.

He was surprised a fortnight later to have a further visit. This time it was the congregation servant accompanied by the head circuit servant for that Australian state. Despite their position and their years of study, David confidently opened his marked Bible again, and gave concrete, Scriptural reasons for his new faith.

"Return to the Society," they warned, "or you will be entirely cut off from us. No member will be allowed to speak to you or associate with you in any way."

David courageously replied, "I am sorry, but I now know the Watchtower does not have the truth. I could never return. Furthermore, I shall work for every Jehovah's Witness I can find and share with them the truth that means so much to me."

In all, fifteen months had passed between the day Bob first called on David and Brenda and the day that he baptized them. Nanna had been baptized in the meantime.

One day when Bob was visiting at "Blue Gums," John said, "We've been in the Adventist Church for some time now. Looking back, we have only one regret about joining the church when we did."

"What is that?" Bob asked.

"That we did not know about it sooner." John grinned. "Now Valmai is at the Seventh-day Adventist college, Mary will go next, and finally Gary. But how we wish we had come into the church sooner! Then David and Clarice could have enjoyed the benefits the church has for its young people."

"Look at this." Lorna pulled a paper out of an envelope and handed it to Bob. "We've waited over twelve months for these."

"What is it, Mum?" Bob was curious.

"It is our papers of disfellowshipment from the Society, signed by the congregation servant, his assistant, and the Bible-study servant. The reason given is that we have broken our 'Dedication Vows to serve Jehovah as a faithful Witness.'"

"When I became a Witness, I vowed I would serve Jehovah and obey His truth. You know, that was a good vow, and I intend to keep it! That's why I have left the Watchtower, to keep the commandments of Jehovah and serve my Lord and Saviour, Jesus Christ. I have no regrets except that, like John, I didn't know the truth sooner. I thank God that He brought me into the Adventist family, and I trust that the experience I have had will help others who, in their search for the channel of truth, may find the right answer to the question, 'Is it the Watchtower?'"

15

After Many Days

More than thirty years have passed since the experiences recorded in this book. "Blue Gums" and the neighboring farm of Betty and Norm have long been sold. In their retirement both families once again found themselves attending the same Adventist church. The friendship made all those years ago held many wonderful memories as they recounted the way the Lord had led and blessed them through the years.

David and Brenda are still very active Adventists. For many years David has held major positions of responsibility in the congregation including that of senior elder. After he became an Adventist he continued to have difficulties at that factory with shift work. Shortly afterwards he was offered work with a bakery which did not work on the Sabbath. He accepted it believing the Lord was leading him. This then led him to buy his own bakery business, which down through the years provided him and Brenda with a good income to support and rear their five children.

When he left the factory his work mates bitterly ridiculed him. However, they were soon to envy David. Shortly afterwards an economic recession hit the country and this factory was sold. They found themselves without employment, but David's business was flourishing. David believed the Lord had more than blessed and rewarded him for his faithfulness.

Through the years, Bob Watson has visited and kept in touch with them all. On January 23, 1982, they had a reunion in the little bush church where this story began. The church was packed for the occasion. Lorna and John sat in the front seat, as Bob Watson preached the morning sermon. Betty Anderson sang as she did all those years ago when Lorna and John were baptized. In the afternoon, experiences were recounted of the events which took place at that time, most of which have been recorded briefly in this book.

It was a deeply moving occasion for Loma to be surrounded by so many members of her family and friends who with her had left Watchtower teachings to accept Jesus Christ as their personal Saviour and follow Bible truth. As she looked at them she wondered what may have happened if they had never made that decision at that time? She thought of the hundreds of thousands of loyal Jehovah's Witnesses who had been led to believe the End was coming in 1975.[1] When this date proved to be but another false prophecy and erroneous teaching of the Watchtower Society, thousands of these very sincere Witnesses left the organization bewildered and bereft of any faith. Most believed there was no other organization that they could join where they could find Bible truth and happiness in serving the Lord. Lorna realized it could have happened to them. With deep gratitude and praise she thanked God for His wonderful love and leading. In the Adventist church they had found joy, peace and above all, salvation.

On December 29, 1990, Lorna and John celebrated their 60th wedding anniversary. Bob Watson returned for the occasion. On that Sabbath morning, Betty Anderson played the organ, and Bob preached the sermon. Lorna sat in a wheel chair alongside John. It was a very happy occasion, but it was to be the last time that they were ever to attend church together.

Before Bob returned to his home in a distant state in Australia he visited Lorna. Both knew it would be the last time they would see each other in this life. However, Lorna's voice and faith was as strong as ever. Her face glowed as she spoke of the personal and loving relationship she had with her Saviour. A relationship that had grown more wonderful with the passing of the years.

Bob told her that more than 300,000 copies of this story had now been published in many different languages world-wide and had led thousands to find the Truth. "It is going to take you the whole Millennium to meet them all," Bob smiled.

Lorna shook her head, "I find it hard to believe that the Lord should have used my humble experience to that

[1]   *(See Appendix concerning 1975)

extent," she said. "I am just grateful He graciously saved me from the errors of the Watchtower Society and led me into His wonderful truth."

A few weeks later the doctor told Lorna that her life was rapidly coming to a close. That night she was taken into hospital. By the next afternoon the last member of her family had arrived at her bedside. In a clear voice she spoke to each one of her loved ones urging them to be faithful and ready to meet her on the resurrection morning when Christ returns.

Her last witness was similar to the Apostle Paul who said, "I have fought a good fight,....I have kept the faith: henceforth there is laid up for me a crown of righteousness, which the Lord, the righteous judge, shall give me at that day: and not to me only, but unto all them also that love his appearing." 2 Timothy 4:7,8.

APPENDIX

A. Some of the Watchtower Publications which suggested the End would come in 1975:

"The Watchtower", August 15, 1968, pages 494–501:

WHY ARE YOU LOOKING FORWARD TO **1975?**

"The Watchtower", May 1, 1968, pages 270–277:

MAKING WISE USE *Of The Remaining Time*

"The Kingdom Ministry", May 1974 Commended those *"selling their homes and property"* to go into the pioneer service to *"spend the short time remaining before the wicked world's end."*

"Life Everlasting - In Freedom of the Sons of God", (1966) Page 29:

....] According to this trustworthy Bible chronology six thousand years from man's creation will end in 1975, and the seventh period of a thousand years of human history will begin in the fall of 1975 C.E.
⁴² So six thousand years of man's existence on earth will soon be up, yes, within this generation.

B. Jehovah's Witness & Seventh-day Adventist Membership Growth 1960–1995

When the end did not come to pass in 1975 as expected, thousands of loyal Jehovah's Witnesses left the Watch Tower Society, bitterly disappointed and bewildered.

This graph shows how it affected the membership growth.

Before 1975, Witnesses had experience a similar growth and membership increase.

The Witnesses have never recovered their losses due to the 1975 date failure. From 1976 until 1980 there was almost no membership growth.

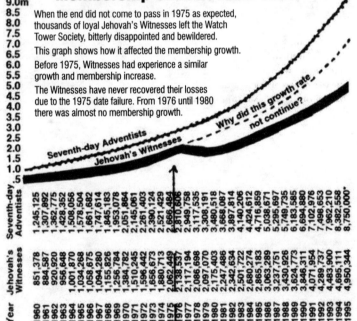

Year	Jehovah's Witnesses	Seventh-day Adventists
1960	851,378	1,245,125
1961	884,587	1,307,892
1962	920,920	1,362,775
1963	956,648	1,428,352
1964	1,001,870	1,508,056
1965	1,034,268	1,578,504
1966	1,058,675	1,661,682
1967	1,094,280	1,747,614
1968	1,155,826	1,845,183
1969	1,256,784	1,953,078
1970	1,384,782	2,051,864
1971	1,510,245	2,145,061
1972	1,596,442	2,261,403
1973	1,656,673	2,390,124
1974	1,880,713	2,521,429
1975	2,062,449	2,666,484
1976	2,138,537	2,810,506
1977	2,117,194	2,949,758
1978	2,086,698	3,117,535
1979	2,097,070	3,308,191
1980	2,175,403	3,480,518
1981	2,247,486	3,668,087
1982	2,342,634	3,897,814
1983	2,501,722	4,140,206
1984	2,680,274	4,424,612
1985	2,865,183	4,716,859
1986	3,063,289	5,038,671
1987	3,237,751	5,295,697
1988	3,430,926	5,749,735
1989	3,624,773	6,183,585
1990	3,846,311	6,694,880
1991	4,071,954	7,102,976
1992	4,289,737	7,498,653
1993	4,483,900	7,962,210
1994	4,695,111	8,382,558
1995	4,950,344	8,750,000*

We'd love to send you a free catalog of titles we publish or even hear your thoughts, reactions, criticism, about things you did or didn't like about this

or any other book we publish.

Just contact us at:

TEACH Services, Inc.
1-800/367-1844

or

www.TEACHServices.com